I'm Not Waving, I'm Drowning

I'm Not Waving,
I'm Drowning

Surviving Bipolar Illness

Salvina Cappello

To order additional copies of this book, contact:
Xlibris Corporation
1-888-795-4274
www.Xlibris.com
Orders@Xlibris.com
31074

CONTENTS

Caveat

Although my illness was especially sensitive to antidepressant inducement, anti-depressant drugs are life savers for some bipolars and many unipolars. (people that only exhibit depression)

When you pass through the waters they will
not sweep over you.

Isaiah 43:2

It has been said that once you travel through
deep waters . . . . only then can you really
help others . . . . it's the "been there and done
that" thing!

Salvina

Come what may, time and the hour runs
through the roughest day.

MacBeth III 146-147

This book is in loving memory of Eleanor; I called her Mama.

Eleanor lived for 30 years with this illness not stabilized.

She encouraged me to "go the distance". She died of bipolar affective disorder in her sixties.

She put up a good fight to survive.

At the National Institutes of Health (NIH), when they announced her death, I was on "eye contact" for severe biological depression.

I ran from the day room crying and shouting "Mama!"

"Mama!" "No, no."

"How did she do it?" I asked Dr. C.

He answered, "She hung herself in the basement."

"She loved life as much as I do. People will never understand that she did not want to die," I said.

Dr. C responded, "You are right, Salvina. People will not understand. They still do not understand bipolar illness.

I promised myself on that day that, if I got better, I would help them understand that Eleanor did not want to die. She was a survivor and so am I. She loved life as much as I do.

. . . and also in loving memory of my beloved dad . . . . whom I loved very much; he was always there for me. I just wish that he understood the truth about this illness in his lifetime. While he was very proud of me, in many ways about this he was ashamed, and let me know it. He was still the best dad anyone could have.

. . . to my aunt . . . . my mother's sister, who lived and died never knowing what hit her . . . . non-functional most of her adult life . . . suffering in a generation with little knowledge.

. . . . to my mom . . . who denied the illness for most of my adult life, but has recently become very supportive and has joined the ranks pushing for more for public awareness.

PERSONAL PREFACE (2005)

This is a story about my struggle with manic-depression, or bipolar disorder, the preferred medical term. I want to share with you how it affected my life in the hope that others would be spared my horrible experiences.

I have known many losses. The first to go was my family. My marriage never should have happened, but the disorder caused me to be afraid not to go through with it. My fine career was another casualty of the disorder. But the greatest losses caused by the disorder were some very special and talented friends, some who did not understand it and others who died from it.

When bipolar illness is episodic, the symptoms can seem like bizarre behavioral anomalies, but in reality they are biological.

In the down phase of the cycle, I lose all motor function and ability to walk and talk. I have no appetite and I always feel as though something awful has taken control of my body; as though I am dying. I have no libido and sounds and smells are accentuated, especially the stench of my inability to take care of myself in these extreme states.

The high phase, though, is especially offensive to most people. My latest six-year struggle was started by repeated sleep disruption (insomnia). The general public often exacerbated my highs by doing things contrary to what would be prescribed. When I started cycling up or going into the high phase, people around me were unable to effectively intervene. They were scared.

In the high, one surely leaves a wake behind one. This disorder affects relationships, finances and just about everything in life. I bought a beautiful trousseau and did not even have a boyfriend, in each manic episode. Spending is a symptom of the high phase. This physical illness is to the brain much like diabetes is to the pancreas.

I have lived through three years of rapid cycling illness, up and down, never well. This is the most critical form of the disorder. Then came three more years with less frequent episodes. I felt extremely isolated. Only now am I beginning to establish a support base again. But I feel as though I were reborn. I am not fighting the battles of the past. All I want is for others who suffer from it to learn from my experiences and for all of you who have not experienced it, to learn how you can help us better. When we call out to you, we really need your help!

This is my story.

Looking Through a Kaleidoscope

I arrived in midtown Manhattan late at night and all the buildings were melting into one another . . . like a Salvador Dali picture. I parked the car illegally and got out into the pouring rain. I barely noticed the rain as I was intent to find Daniel and run away with him. I turned the corner running towards the all too familiar skyscraper and just waited for him across the street. It continued to rain . . . no umbrella . . . no raincoat . . . just the desire to see him again. I was certain we were running away together and would be living happily ever after. Isn't that the way The Little Mermaid ended? He did not show up that night. But I did not give up. I went back to my car, parked it legally, and stayed in a hotel for the night. Perhaps he would just know enough to show up here. With all this rain; I could imagine myself a real mermaid that night.

I like to think I am normal or as normal as any person can be. I feel most comfortable on the Upper West Side of Manhattan, I guess that labels me a little bit off center. The West side is reserved for creative types, and manic-depression or bipolar illness is reserved for creative types, too.

Aside from causing periodic abnormalities, pre-menopausal and sleep disorder symptoms welcomed me with a humdinger of a Little Mermaid and West Side Story episode.

Let us begin at the beginning . . . .

I was attending school and living in a small town in Pennsylvania. I was holding a cum laude average when I started to cycle up. I started displaying symptoms of the high, like being very candid about the people around me. You can always believe a manic because we lose censorship control. One cannot tell a lie from that mood state. It always burns bridges and you usually regret it afterwards. Things were escalating. I was not feeling well and no one was trying to intervene and help. I was in incredible pain and I felt terribly lonely because hardly anyone would talk to me. I became an outcast in, and disenfranchised from, the school in general. They really had no understanding of my disorder and they were scared of me.

I began to feel afraid to sleep in my apartment. I was convinced someone was infecting it with dangerous fumes. At times I rented a local hotel room or found a pickup truck to sleep in. I was lucky that I didn't get shot during this time. One morning a couple found me in their truck. I thought they were going to call the police. I told them that I was afraid to sleep in my home and they were so nice, they just directed me home. If I went too long without treatment nowadays, paranoia would accompany my episode.

One day, I thought I smelled smoke. I called 911 and asked for the fire department. They searched everything and even broke down a door to make sure that nothing was coming out. The whole fire department of this small town arrived to greet me and nothing was wrong.

I was called into a confrontational meeting at school. You should never confront someone in the high phase; it only exacerbates the moodswings. The meeting only convinced me that we were living out The Little Mermaid and I was on the way to losing my voice. One woman in the group was a striking Ursula, in my eyes at the time. She even lied to cover up something that she did, which made my life harder, maybe impossible on campus. A boldface lie. I was stunned.

Soon after that I went back into the field behind my apartment and I was sure I was getting directions from my would be prince, directions on how to find him. I walked through this field all night one night, injured by the brush and all muddy from the stream. My fear was becoming so great that I did not want to stay in the area anymore. One very nice lady out there would check in on me. She knew I was going through something. Michelle drove several hours to try to get me medical help. I was not suicidal or homicidal, but I was unwilling to sign myself in. I was scared. I could not legally be committed, but I needed help.

Michelle's efforts were in vain. I returned to the apartment and left again at once. I stopped near my mom's beach house and checked into a motel for a few days. I thought maybe we will meet here, but we did not. I was sure there would be an encounter. I bought a few things. It was absolutely real to me that other people were trying to kill me. Across the street from my home there is a house that looks almost haunted at night. It reminded me of 101 Dalmatians. These fairy tales were all overlapping with the same theme: finding Daniel, soon. I was drinking water like it was going out of style. My mother, to whom I paid a visit, was no help. I felt like Gregor Samsa from Kafka's Metamorphosis, a person who turned into a cockroach in his bed. She would not take me to the hospital. It was an imposition on her busy day.

Then came the drive to New York. Daniel was a high level executive at a major network, which made it into A West Side Story for me. This was all so real to me, so very real. We would be together forever at last. I kept traveling back and forth hoping to find him. During the day, I would shop. I was down to almost no money in the New York Grand Hyatt, ordering expensive room service, usually salmon; I actually secured two rooms, one for Daniel and one for me. I did not have a lot of belongings as I kept leaving them behind. Thus I lost a beautiful Gucci white gold watch and a great winter coat, but most of all, for a short period of time, I lost my mind. I was not really crazy, but clearly out of it.

I was waiting for Daniel to come, oblivious to any of the people back home that might be concerned. Apparently, there was a major search for me in progress. Michelle had a list of contacts in New York and was working with my family to try to track me down. They did have a good pulse on me and were not far behind. My mother had given me an EZ—pass, which helped my brother find out that I had gone to New York. My car was taken in by the police and my brother found me at the Hyatt. I did not want to see him. He came up to my room with NYPD policemen who were threatening to break down the door if I did not open it. I was so scared, so disappointed that they found me before Daniel. This was not how it was supposed to happen!

My brother took me to a local hospital where my mother came to meet me. This episode clearly shook her. She feared that someone may have murdered me or that I might have disappeared in a homeless shelter. This time more than ever before she realized that I was sick.

In the emergency room I was agitated and kept wanting to get up and walk away. The security wanted to put me in restraints, but my mother told them to please leave me alone because I am never violent. In my mind, however, they were out to kill me, and I fantasized that Daniel would come to rescue me here and we would live happily ever after.

I was taken behind closed doors and my mother had to answer a lot of questions. They put me in a non-voluntary ward for the first time in my life though I was neither violent nor suicidal. What was going on here? I refused to take medication, so they locked me in. It was really scary. Some patients were in transfer to state hospitals. They could do anything to me now. I was no longer in control. What was my future now at fifty?

Even here I was expecting to encounter Daniel. I was still oblivious to most of the world around me. I kept wanting to see Daniel. I heard him talking to me. He said we would be leaving for South America, where nobody could bother us. Every night I waited for him to come. But Daniel never came. All the time, I was driving to find Daniel. We had millions of dollars and places to go before we slept, I thought. My libido was ready to meet him, too. But at least I did not have an affair. I am always attracted to someone during an episode, but I have not had an affair for years now. And I never even called Daniel.

The final reality comes with a striking blow. All those bridges burnt, all that time lost, all that money wasted. The disappointment is unbearable. The awakening from this state is heartbreaking. Daniel didn't come. He will never come. When reality hits, that's when the down phase begins for me.

I hate the hospitals, but sometimes you need them. One night about three staff members came in and said: "You are taking this medication or we are going to inject it into you." The medicine sedated me. In a high state, this drug is good for temporary relief. One doctor suggested that I stay on it for maintenance. No way, I thought. I would never function again if I do so.

I did not want to talk to anyone. Where can I go to stay? I still had my apartment in Pennsylvania, but I was too heavily medicated to take care of myself. A family close to me took me in for a week. They could tell I was heavily medicated. I returned to Pennsylvania and started a new life for myself.

I have always had the impression that a professor and a counselor at my Pennsylvania school had little or no knowledge of what I was going through at this time. It is not humorous. It can be a killer in both the high and the low phase. I know that they do not view it as a real illness but instead as part of a liberal agenda. I wish it were not real. This kind of counsel is deadly counsel and should be reconsidered very carefully. Some circles need to reconsider this position because without treatment, people can die!

This book is written not only for diagnosed bipolars and treating doctors, but also, or rather especially, for the general public, in the wish that you all gain a deeper insight into the illness beyond its definition as a chemical imbalance and its stereotypization. At times, my own family treated me like I was contagious. We who have the bi-polar illness are not.

Why did it take four months to control what could have been controlled in one week? I was too sick to get the help myself and people are not yet educated enough to know how to help. My friend Michelle always knows when I am in the high phase and tries to intervene. If she can intervene, so can anyone else. For me, parts of my life have been pinnacles of success and other parts have been an uphill battle to lick it and live a relatively normal life. My illness encompassed every possible snag. I have more motivation than ever to tell this story. I want future generations to encounter fewer problems, and they will if they understand more. Now let us travel back in time, to my childhood.

I was born on June 7, 1952 in a suburb of New Jersey.

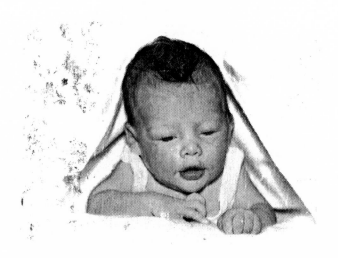

CHAPTER 1

A Big Fish in a Little Pond

I was gazing out the window of our apartment that was on the third floor of my father's parents' home. There were all these lights flashing and they were carrying my grandmother out on a stretcher. This is my first memory of life. I was afraid for grandma. I turned around to my mom and asked her what was happening:

"Where are they taking grandma?" I questioned. I kept getting words of reassurance that everything was okay, but the commotion around me suggested otherwise. Grandma had another heart attack, one of several that she would have the rest of her life. My grandmother lived through this heart attack. I did not yet know how much I would come to love this woman after whom I was named. My grandparents' home was a big Victorian that sat high up on the hill of a small industrial town in the northeastern United States. It was a perfect home in which children could play. There were great fort-making hills and we would tumble down the hills with great ease and fun. The home was built originally for a mistress of a doctor and it had a rose garden across the street. It was perfect for family gatherings and get-togethers of all sorts.

About the time I was three years old, we moved into our own Victorian home down the street from my paternal grandparents. I remember the day we moved in, to some extent, because this blond girl around my age came over and was getting in between the legs of all the movers. She was very curious about the new children moving just two doors down from her home. Her name was Carrie and we were to become best friends even through high school.

In my family, all the babies were born with dark brown and curly hair, but we all had fair skin color. I understood nothing about ethnic differences. I did not understand that there was anything different about us. We were living in an Anglo-Saxon Protestant neighborhood.

The town was a mining and industrial town during the Revolutionary War. While my world-view of the neighborhood was myopic, other neighborhoods were more diverse in composition. Today the town is very diverse with a considerable Hispanic influx.

If we were not welcome in this little town, we were definitely accepted, due to my grandfather's success. We were welcomed by all the town's shopkeepers as our whole family was good for paying our bills. My grandfather Nanu was a pioneer in his own right. Nanu transported his whole family from Sicily right into the American dream. The American dream really worked for him. My father's father was a smart businessman. Recently, a family friend remembered driving into New York City with my father and grandfather and my grandfather turned around and told her:

"I come to the United States not two nickels to rub together in my pocket and I make a load."

It is true. He started a pocketbook factory and then a garment factory where my dad and his brothers also worked. Carrie was always with us, although it was evident by her blond hair and blue eyes that she was not born into our family. She began to refer to herself as my parents' fifth daughter. To the credit of her family, they never mentioned our differences. In fact, it was clear that there was no discrimination on their part.

Every week, my mom made homemade tomato sauce. She would always find these little holes in the sauce where Carrie had plucked out the meatballs. She made much of a fuss over it, but she probably rather enjoyed that Carrie really appreciated her meatballs.

Carrie was pretty bold. We always shared family vacations together. Carrie would join my family's vacations, and my older sister and I would always join her family at their summer home in a northern state. We were very active there, including fishing with a local fisherman named Collin. Collin was like a grandfather to all of us. He really enjoyed all of us; you could just tell that he was doing all of this from his heart.

I remember once Collin had several of us in his pickup truck. I was up front in the cabin with Collin. One of the kids in the back seat threw an apple at an oncoming truck and hit it. The truck turned around and chased Collin until he stopped. He was yelling up a storm. Collin never said a word. After the man left, Collin turned around and looked at me and said: "Man were a bit peeved, weren't he?" I just smiled at his composure and patience with all of us. Carrie's parents and grandparents would often end the day with drinking, a difference from my home. I did learn a lot from Carrie's parents about morals and other things, too. I spent hours with them. Her father was especially good about teaching us moral values like not to litter, speed or gossip.

Even though my dad did not graduate high school, he was no slouch when it came to history and politics. He fought in WW II and was proud to be an American. He was on the USS Ticonderoga when a kamikaze pilot bombed it. His life was spared by minutes. He had a profound influence on my life. Since his death in 1994, my life was never quite the same.

I came from a family with six children and I was the second to oldest child. I must say that to me it seemed as if there were three older children and three younger children, almost like two separate families.

Growing up, it seemed as though I had the Midas touch: everything I touched turned to gold—academics, sports, theatrics, and relationships. Of his six children, my dad made it subliminally clear, I showed the most promise.

My father often encouraged me to become an attorney. In retrospect, I would have made a good attorney. Had he not pushed it so intensely, I may have come to it on my own. My mother was raised in a city ghetto and "married up." My dad was accustomed to having money. I suppose my mom was too often reminded of her background. She always told us that we were born with a silver spoon in our mouths.

My mother was a beautiful young woman and I also believe that my dad saw her as a good mother and wife. She was the youngest of five children, perhaps the cutest, too. They had a difficult life and my mother says that the older siblings had sacrificed a lot for her. Due to poverty, her older sisters had to join the work force at an early age. Her father suffered battle fatigue (a.k.a "shell shock") in World War I, and he had to be institutionalized.

I do not believe that the marriage between my mom and dad was ideal. My dad loved nature and boating. Mom did not like either one. Dad cared about all his children, whereas mom had her favorites, particularly one of my younger brothers. While she worried about appearances, I think, dad was very down to earth. The family had great expectations of this beautiful young woman; they wanted her to obtain a future insurance policy, and she did.

My mom and dad married when she was only eighteen years old. My grandfather paid for a Cinderella-type wedding for her. My grandmother on my mother's side died early at the age of 60 . . . . from a difficult and sacrificial life and rheumatic fever.

My mother must have felt as though she died and went to heaven on that day of her wedding. Her own father was not at the wedding and her brother walked her down the aisle. Anyone would want to escape the ghetto life and survive. She still works hard for a seventy-four year old woman. But she married well . . . . very well.

Mom says that she learned about loyalty from her mother who visited her sick husband every weekend with some of the children. And in fact, when it came to meeting practical needs, mom was very dedicated. She saw that we were well fed and clothed. She even ironed our socks! She was probably overworked and felt unappreciated-

We were all spoiled and did not have to do much house work. She is such a domestic perfectionist-a Martha Stewart before her time, that I had to find other avenues to succeed. She was the mother with the most innovation as a room mother, as a Girl Scout leader, as a car-pool driver. She had good ideas. She was at all our events from football games to ski competitions to ballet. She wanted to see us succeed, an extension of herself. I did succeed, through education and a very good and rewarding career. In the house, though, nothing any of us did suited her fancy.

She probably loved her mother more than anyone in the world. Her mother had a difficult life, raising five children alone during the depression. My mother relates stories of her cooking for the family and waiting until all the children were finished before eating the leftovers.

My mom had the one sister who was institutionalized most of her adult life. She had clearly been over-medicated and put into a back ward. I believe she actually had bipolar illness, but this was not known at the time. One picture that I have of her would suggest that she might have been the most beautiful of the sisters in my mom's family.

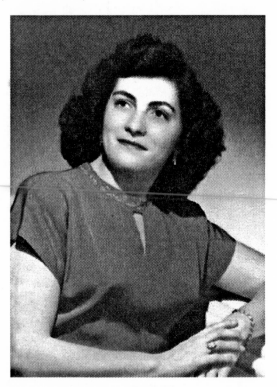

I suppose it is because of her that my discharge records from a local well-known Ivy League hospital on February 6, 1985, states: "Family history is positive for affective disorder." It is after all, a genetic disease. I sometimes wonder what pain my aunt had to endure. I saw how the vast majority of people treated her virtually like a doorknob, family, sadly like a non-person.

When the time came for my confirmation (I was raised Catholic), I wanted this aunt to be my godmother, but mom said that she was unable to do it. Perhaps, if the family had not given up on her, she would not have lived such a horrific life. They did not understand then what they know now. She would most likely not have been functional anyhow, but I will always remember her with that blank stare caused by drugs and the stigma. The drugs are better today, but the stigma remains. I guess this is why my mother had been in denial about my illness for so long. She must have feared that it all came from her side of the family. It didn't.

My parents started a family right away. My mom woke up by 5 a.m. every morning. She squeezed natural orange juice and always tended to us. She wanted us always perfectly dressed. I suppose that was another way of compensating for her past poverty. She had the reputation in the community of being a very good mother. She was always on top of everything that was going on. She must have been subconsciously pushed to perfection by my father as well as by her own need to overcome the past. Perhaps this is why my eventual illness became so problematic for her. It brought back to life the problems of her sister and father. She did the best that she could. "The illness" is something to haunt her and it could not be easily rationalized away. She loved her mom and her mom had wisdom. Now I realize how true was what my grandmother always told my mother: "Believe none of what you hear and only half of what you think you see." My father's family had enough generations of comfort to be considered "old money." My father never felt the need to flash his wealth. You would never even know that he had money. He was comfortable driving around in a jalopy and wearing the clothes of a laborer.

Recently I learned that the disorder exists on both sides of the family. Denial is an easy out. For the longest time my family's attitude towards "it" was complete denial and no willingness to learn about it. When I had an episode mom would say things like "You are probably just really burned out," or "You are probably just going through early menopause, it runs in our family!"

All these reactions would infuriate me; has my family not been told what I had, over and over again? I was suffering and lonely day after day. I guess in my aunt's generation people accepted whatever the doctor said. Let me tell you: there are good doctors and bad doctors. I fought my way to life! I had to live a full life. My mother is just beginning to open up and read about it. She recently said : "Everyone has the same symptoms; it must be a real illness." This day was my most joyous day: finally my mother recognized my condition!

Let's go back to the man that started it all: Nanu. He was not about bipolar illness, but the about American dream and the Cappello family. I remember my grandfather, Nanu, my father's father, because he always had a stern look on his face and was always holding a gray Wall Street book in his hand with all the numbers. His wife was very maternal. I loved to go and sit and talk to grandma. None of her grandchildren could do any wrong. They were the typical patriarch and matriarch. They were real anchors for me during my childhood.

My dad was very close to his father, and he also was a real anchor for all of us, too. At his funeral, a nephew eulogized him saying, "He was always there for me." Truthfully, he was always there for all of us. He did not understand my illness and was embarrassed about it, but at least he tried and never abandoned me. He promised me that I will always have a roof over my head and food at his home. Always.

My parents were very responsible about raising children and rarely left us alone. Dad had to go to New York City every day to make deliveries in the garment district. He was a manufacturer of ladies' clothing. I often went with him. We would make a stop at the brokerage firm. I remember that the secretaries there would always treat me nicely and give me jelly candies. As I grew older, I came to appreciate the perks of getting free garments, as any woman would. I remember the vendors with hot pretzels and hot dogs. My dad would always stop to buy a hot dog; he loved them.

There was something about New York City that seemed so big to a small child, the tall buildings and the skyline and all the crazy traffic. Let's face it, New York City is a city like no other city. I guess I was a "daddy's girl." My father loved Manhattan as I would also come to love Manhattan later in life.

My dad's extended family was very close. We used to get together even with second and third cousins all the time. We had annual reunions in upstate New York. I felt a bond with my dad's family. Most of them had been to college. Of course, they had their share of family feuds as well, and when they fight, they fight. The only one who tried to give everyone a fair chance was Uncle Bobby, dad's first cousin, my second cousin and one of dad's best friends. He is a hard worker and a good man. When Uncle Bobby is around, things are always lively. He has a terrific sense of humor. I remember one night, when I was newly married, he called with a faked voice and told me that I had won the lottery. He did such a good job that I believed it for a moment, even though I did not even have a lottery ticket in hand. He has five children all of whom have done well for themselves. In the later years, Uncle Bobby had all the family reunions on his property. He was the relative that gave me emotional support at the death of my dad.

My father claimed to be an atheist right up until he died. The bone of contention was always the Catholic church. Dad saw in it nothing but hypocrisy, while mom wanted to go every day and knew every priest in a ten-mile radius. Most of the Cappello family has a problem with anything religious. We are for the most part agnostics or atheists. Dad referred to priests as "black coats" and he was not at all complimentary. My dad was a real character at times. A lot of people were afraid of his brusque persona, but he was a real teddy bear. He scared me too, but I was also the sole person who dared to confront him regularly about women's rights and the like. He liked my spunky personality. From an early age I was interested in world events. We would have political debates maybe from when I was in sixth grade. I felt sort of estranged from my peers in elementary school. We were not on the same page; they seemed to me so immature!

There was frequent tension over religious education in the household. This must have caused my mom a lot of pain. However, mom won the religious battle. We attended catechism and weekly mass, but we did not to go to a Catholic day school or let "this thing" get out of perspective. Dad wanted to keep it in control lest any of us kids would want to become a priest or a nun. I spent a lot of time with my dad. I remember being in restaurants where he would always bring up in conversation what a good lawyer I would make. I definitely could not be a doctor. I could not stand the sight of blood. Little did I know how much blood I would have to see my lifetime, including my own!

My father tried to direct all his children towards higher education, which he had not had the opportunity to obtain.

Bipolars have a heightened emotional sensitivity; many of us are in creative vocations, such as artists and entertainers. When I was in grammar school, I was a sensitive child. I was the only child in the whole school who would cry at the end of every school year. Somehow I must have sensed that things would never be the same again. I recall my playtime. I played teacher a lot on my back porch, a very demanding play teacher. This level of expectations would follow me into my career in television, but I never asked from others for more than I required from myself.

My high school years were effortless and I was waiting to be challenged by something in college. Languages came with special ease for me. In high school, I was taking Chinese, Spanish and French as well as an accelerated math schedule. I was a cheerleader, a gymnast and even a budding thespian. Mom was the force behind all these activities. She also took us to the stores and bought us seasonal wardrobes. We were so polished.

I was a social chameleon. No matter what the social strata or ethnic background, I seemed to find a way to bond with just about anyone. I guess that is why even the so-called "nerds" liked me. I did not treat them meanly, even though I was part of the "in" crowd. That exuberance sometimes caused me trouble with men who misinterpreted my friendly and naïve attitude.

I was always at the top of my class. Like my dad, I loved nature. Even my mother to this day says: "You are your father's daughter".

We had two homes on an upscale beach resort. Dad would come down on weekends in the summer. I can remember soaking up the sun and having him sneak up on me and pull me by the feet down into the water. There was a special father-daughter relationship there. It did not stop me from being rebellious as a young adult, however.

I began to develop close friendships with people with similar interests. Peter was the son of a doctor and family friend. We started to spend a lot of time together. He was an expert skier, he played guitar and sang folk songs and he loved to go to parks, to walk and fly kites. We spent so much time together that both families thought we would marry. I knew it was nothing more than friendship. I had no romantic interest in Peter at all. I suspect the same was true for him. One day dad dropped Peter and me off in Manhattan for a day in the city. He said: "Now be sure you do not go to 42nd Street." Well, that was the first place we went; I did not know it was the red light district then.I did not even know what the red light district was. This would turn out to be a pattern in my life. "Don't do it!" meant "I have to find out why!"

Whether it was winter, spring, summer or fall, each season held something special for me. In the fall, there were rides in the country to see the changing leaves and pick hickory nuts; in the winter I could not wait for those good snowfalls in order to hit the ski slopes. Those great ski moments in Vermont: Stratton and Bromley were especially treasured. It was a rush and the scenery was lovely. The spring; well every spring held a rebirth of sorts for me. Everything fresh and anew and invigorating; that would become even more so due to the illness in my adult life. In the summer, we always spent time at our beach home. It was great! I loved the ocean; to walk; to swim; to be. The ocean was an escape for me, then. It still is, but only in the early morning or at night, without all the tourists who come to soak in the sun.

One of my earliest poems was about the sea and it went something like this:

The Sea

I want to be by the sea . . .

chasing seagulls through

the marshmallow clouds at dawn

and to be inside each wave . . . .

as it gently breaks on shore and

mingles with the sand.

However, the driver was not only the son of a good family friend, but an Italian. His dad talked my dad into it, but somehow my dad turned out to be right. I wish he wasn't. There were several of us going, maybe two boys and four girls. When we were nearing our destination and still on the Massachusetts Turnpike, Fred decided that he wanted to change drivers while the car was on automatic pilot and it was raining. I was the only one sitting in the car with enough sense to say: "I don't think this is a good idea."

Daredevil Fred had to test fate. I just remember flying over the embankment and the car flipping over and over again. We finally stopped just before we hit a group of trees. I think we were all somewhat knocked unconscious for a bit. The week before, Carrie's mom had told me: "If you are ever in a car wreck, make sure you turn off the ignition, so the car doesn't blow up." I woke up and started screaming to turn off the ignition. She probably saved our lives. The car had been totaled and I had black and blue marks all over my body. They would not be easily explained away. I was so disgusted that I just turned around and went home.

This was my first cognizant brush with death and it began a long spiritual journey about the meaning of life. At this point in my life, I started reading a lot of Jean Paul Sartre, Camus and Kafka and all the existentialists. I was really trying to understand the purpose of life. In an empty bathtub at night, I made the rounds of these writers with a special understanding of No Exit by Jean Paul Sartre. After all, I did not ask to be born. What if there is some judgment later? I never asked to be born. Why was I born now and not during some other time? Nothing made sense to me at this time in my life, but I was really starting to question everything.

One friend of mine thought it was all very simple: "You simply live, and then you die," he said. Somehow inside myself I knew there had to be something more than that. I just did not know what. These books were a macabre bedtime companion.

Going to church for me was like standing up and saying the pledge of allegiance. It did not offer anything about eternity for me. How could one just be fortunate enough to be born into salvation at birth by being one denomination or another and getting baptized? God had to be an equal opportunity deity. My search would continue for some time. At that time, I probably was not even convinced of the existence of God yet. I was kind of agnostic. I researched language schools and opted to go to a prestigious university that specializes in languages and foreign affairs. I decided to study Chinese because it would offer more of a challenge than the Romance languages. I was admitted to the university early. All indicators predicted a great and fulfilling life! I was a BIG FISH IN A LITTLE POND. The only thing I would miss are the ski slopes!

CHAPTER 2

Leveling Out The Playing Field

With my love for politics and international affairs, a major cosmopolitan city and a prestigious university were seemingly a perfect fit for me. Oftentimes, one would pass a famous person. I suppose these years made famous people just something that was part of the scenery for me. By the spring of my freshman year, it seemed that the whole of the anti-Vietnam protest would wind up on our campus—10,000 people marching here and camping out on our sports field!

I was always intense and focused about my schoolwork, a super achiever. Yet, when I considered the peace movement, I knew in my heart that it was the moral thing to do. Back to the garden and the greening of the country were good things to consider for me at the time. Equality for women in the workplace seemed like the only right thing to support. I visited several communes in the country outside the city. Communal living looked practical. Let each person use his or her skills. I suppose the idea was adapted from the Israeli kibbutz or moshav. In the end, it was too idealistic. While I pondered all these ethical considerations, my roommate was beginning to activate in her way, in a fun way. "You just have to go and get arrested," said Katherine. "They just put you in the baseball stadium and everyone has a great time!" Why is it that Katherine always made me curious and she came out smelling like a rose while I would get in trouble? We were roommates and both studying Chinese language. She was the baby of seven children and I was one of the older of six. We became very good friends at school and remained good friends until this very day. On the first day of classes, our non-yielding Chinese language teacher made it clear to us that he liked small classes. I suppose he was planning some serious weeding over the next four years. I graduated in Chinese language. Only three out of the original 25 graduated in that major.

The same afternoon that Katherine was getting motivated, 10,000 people showed up on campus. About ten students were shooting the breeze in my room. We had been baking bread for all our visitors.

At this prestigious campus, during my freshman year, exams looked like a war zone. There were helicopters circling overhead, policemen were everywhere and equipped with tear gas. In the middle of all this mess, students were walking with their books to the library to study for exams, business as usual. One might have been a little concerned that there would be a repeat of Kent State right before our very eyes. It was a little scary just to be of college age, wearing blue jeans and living in Washington at that time in history. You were automatically profiled as trouble. Many of our students were carrying out sheets and towels for those who were getting tear gassed in our midst. It was surreal. After all, we were just college students, not monsters!

Katherine was my assigned roommate in my freshman year. Katherine, she definitely is adventurous. All the boys loved her. When my parents visited, they took Katherine to dinner with us and when Katherine's parents visited, they took me to dinner with them. We were both serious students. When I work, I work hard and when I play, I play hard. I loved life and people, in general. I have always loved life! My dad affectionately referred to me as the pied piper of people. I liked everyone and most everyone liked me. A chameleon again?

There was something very stimulating about living in a big city for a girl whose favorite television program at age 11 was public television's "Firing Line," talking heads. Not your typical 11-year-old favorite. I was moved by major political events and genuinely saddened by the assassinations of the Kennedys, Martin Luther King, and Anwar Sadat. My frame of reference at that time was blessed are the peacemakers. I have since come to see that war is sometimes necessary, such as the war in Iraq recently. I still like the path of peace over war, if possible. I had to carry a gas mask too long at a later time in my life to be so naïve to think we need not defend ourselves.

In college, the competition was a lot tougher than at my high school. Almost all the students came from upscale prep schools and I went to a public school in a small industrial town. At last, I felt fairly equal with the playing field. Even still, I could write a paper on just about anything in 24 hours, where it would take others months. This ability allowed for more playtime. I was popular, as I was in high school. In fact, I knew so many people that I often could not study at the university library in undergraduate school; that was set aside as a social event. No, I often traveled across town to a large public library to study. In addition to having anonymity, the library had a lot of character. I loved to study within the walls of this specimen of architecture of antiquity in undergraduate school. I was often in awe of the environment on break time. One thing it afforded me was focused studying. I never ran into anyone I knew. In my freshman year, a group of friends decided to spoof on proms and we decided cohesively to hold an annual goof ball in February. My picture for my first goof ball tells a lot about my personality.

By my sophomore year, I opted to live in a coed dorm in the middle of campus, not a wise choice for someone who is popular and yearns to be anonymous from time to time. The people traffic to and from my room was unbelievable. Even "Please Do Not Disturb" signs did not stop people from bursting into the room. There were days I felt like screaming and other times, I rather enjoyed all the attention this high profile location afforded me.

We (the semi-activists of the day) were genuinely convinced that we could make a better world that we could see an end to hypocrisy and that communal living across the nation could work better than the traditional family method of survival. I saw myself living like this in the future, but the dream ended quickly with the recession in 1974. We all had to work hard and vigorously to survive. We hippies became the yuppies of my generation. Now we belong to the aging population. A lot of what we tried to accomplish backfired on us. The family unit broke down and we see latchkey children in herds. The world is not a better place for the trouble. That is unfortunate.

By my junior year, we started living in coed apartments near the campus. It was stimulating because everyone was smart. Sometimes we would have all night discussions. We all became average fish at this prestigious school. The playing field was leveled off.

Since I was studying Chinese language as a major, I would also delve into Eastern philosophies and history. I took a comparative religions course and especially became interested in Lao Tse, Taoism and The Book of Changes: the Way of Ultimate Reality. This kind of easy flowing philosophy "it is but it cannot be named," "go with the flow" was all very appealing to my mind. "Your goal is creative stillness," or "take the path of least resistance." The concept of yin yang is all intertwined into this philosophy. Opposites are working together to order the universe. I call it a philosophy and not a religion because there is no real explanation for afterlife, other than that one becomes a part of nature. I eventually realized that this could not be the truth.

I could not tolerate recreational drugs the way other students at school could.

Let us remember these were the 70's, but I could not participate to the same degree as my co-students. For my comparative religions exam, I had taken an amphetamine to study. By the time I arrived in class, I was shaking and unable to take the exam. I guess one would call this crashing. The professor let me take a makeup exam and all was well.

I guess by now I had become a veritable Taoist and I was throwing the I Ching or Book of Changes for all my friends. Whatever problems you have, you can just come to my room and we will have a look at it through the eyes of throwing these pennies or yarrow sticks. I had lots of takers in those days. Eastern philosophy was and is popular from the 60's on. But it has changed. Now we are living in an "it's all about me generation." We were idealistic, but what if it had panned out?

And then it happened, around October, my "Black October." I nearly stopped eating. I was so slowed down that I could barely move from my bed and my legs were cramping all the time. The only thing I craved was baked or mashed potatoes. I did not want to see or talk to anyone. Somehow I pushed myself to classes or to do what I absolutely needed to do. Surely, I had gone insane, I thought. For me, this was so strange because I am usually very upbeat and outgoing. What went wrong? Would it be like this forever? All I could think of was suicide. Me??? For me to think of suicide was ridiculous! I could not comprehend what was happening to me. My parents did not believe that there was anything wrong with me. I started to go to a school psychologist who used talk therapy and hypnosis.

Let me tell you, talk therapy for biological depression is like trying to talk someone out of having cancer. In fact, I thought I must be dying of cancer or some other such horrible disease. I often said I must have been bitten by a tsetse fly. I was so thirsty all the time, too. I could not stop drinking water and therefore I always needed to go to the ladies' room. Senses are always affected, too. In the down, sounds are exaggerated to the point where they hurt. The siren of an ambulance pierces the inside of an eardrum as though the noise is coming from inside the ear. How can one escape this? Smell, for me, is also exaggerated in the down phase. I usually do not take very good care of myself in the down phase so I often smelled rotten at those times. I knew this unnamed thing was medical in nature and no one could convince me otherwise. Perhaps, had I stopped this psychological talk therapy and found a doctor that could prescribe medications earlier, my life would not have been quite so volatile.

My parents were not being terribly sympathetic. They did not think this was a real illness. I decided to run away from school with my friend Julie. Julie's family owned a helicopter-producing factory. Her family wanted to teach me how to fly a helicopter. I was not feeling up to it. I knew something that I did not talk about: my motor functions were slowed down, they were not normal. I would be dangerous as a pilot now, so I declined. While in the Midwest it dawned on me that in my state there was no way I would be able to support myself. So I returned to school.

My parents were not horrible people at all. Their denial is not an isolated case. It happens often with this kind of illness. They simply did not understand, just like most people. just like myself earlier.

On February 14, 1972, shortly after I arrived back at school, I met John. I was coming down the steps of the co-ed dorm and he was standing on a landing. He was a blond-haired boy that had a look a lot like a young Jack Nicholas. In fact, his nickname by his friends was "the golden bear." We talked all night on the steps.

By March, I was feeling like myself again! I was also in love, very much in love. Walks by the cherry blossoms and talks under trees on campus, I just assumed that love suited me well and that is why I recovered. I still managed to keep all the academic stuff together. I had no idea at that time that March would become my typical month for recovery in the future (a.k.a. "seasonal moodswings."

At the end of that school year John was going to graduate and he had to make some decisions about his life. John was not particularly motivated; I was. This would eventually become a major source of contention between us. I guess I knew it even then, but because of this unnamed illness, I was too afraid of letting go! Up until this point of my life, I was rarely afraid. This thing was frightening to me!

I truly loved John at first. I loved him very much, you know, that starry-eyed gushy stuff. It felt good. It would turn out to be the first time and last for me—at least up until now. I hope it happens again. Infatuations that cannot be realized do not count, and that happened too many painful times.

John went back to live with his parents for a little while, but he missed me, too. He wanted to be with me. I had another two years before I could finish college. John's father had gotten him a sales job with a good company and I suppose, it would have been better for both of us in the long run had he kept it. But, to his father's dismay, John returned to me.

Later on his father and I would become quite close, but at this point when he did not know me, he saw me as the person that was drawing his son away from a good career and a practical life. John moved back and we started living together. Only, while I was no longer doing any kind of drugs, he still was. We started hanging around more with his friends than mine and doing more what he liked to do than what I had previously liked to do.

John was an avid golfer. He grew up around the country club and golf tournaments. We spent a lot of time both around family and the golf course and country clubs. We were having a good time. We both came from conservative upper middle class families and both families were vehemently opposed to our living together outside of marriage. I did not want to give up the relationship, but I was not ready to commit to marriage. I was really too young for that, but we kept getting pressured to take the big step. I held out for a long time. John was less resistant to our marriage.

John was an unintentional leech. He seemed to believe that he deserved to be kept. In retrospect, there were times in our marriage, in the middle of the winter, when we could not afford oil and he would work all night at the country club hotel, with me sleeping at home bundled in quilts. I'm surprised I was not found frozen to death one morning. I often wondered what he was thinking or if he loved me at all. His extracurricular activities made him oblivious to my needs. Some doctors have suggested that I have trouble expressing my needs to others, a martyr complex perhaps. I am getting better at that. I have always taken the high road and that leaves one on other low roads.

When I arrived back to campus for my junior year, I had to spend a few days with friends until the apartment for Katherine and me was ready. I believed deeply in loyalty. To this day, most of my bosses point out that quality about me. Charles, Katherine's boyfriend was living in the townhouse where John and I were staying for a few days. While Katherine was out of town, he went out with another girl right in front of my very eyes. I said, "Charles, how dare you do this to me! Doing this in front of me is no different than doing this in front of Katherine! Katherine is my best friend!" Katherine and I were so close, you could think we were born from the same egg.

When Katherine returned to campus, we were painting bookshelves in our small basement apartment. Katherine could tell that something was bothering me. She kept asking me what was wrong and I just kept on painting. Then I could no longer hold it back, I told her what happened. She broke up with Charles. I felt between a rock and a hard place over the whole thing!! The virtue of loyalty that I possess would prove to be a blessing and a curse my whole life.

I had developed a rather close friendship with an English professor. He and his family lived across the street from us. I regularly baby-sat his three children that year. I always had such a good time with them and came to love them. The relationship was always platonic. I was also a security guard for building entrances at the university. I was working my other job, when a message was left for me to call Katherine. I knew something was up.

When I got hold of Katherine, I thought she was laughing. She was not. She was shrieking. The English professor's only son was hit and killed by a car that day. It was awful, I guess, and she saw it. I do not think the professor ever really recovered from it. I do know this, I was too upset to even give my condolences or go to the funeral. The next time he saw me, using his usual insight, he said: "Salvina, I know you have been thinking of us. I know it has been hard!" I babysat for the child, but the parent was consoling me and acknowledging the pain he knew I felt, but could not express. It was my ultra-sensitivity that made me unable to communicate at a time like this. I cried for a week every time one of our dogs died. He was aware of my unique sensitivity.

Katherine is uniquely sensitive, too. We are both eclectic, too. We were so much alike in many ways and paired by random selection freshman year. Katherine did know how to play the system better than me, though She knew how to get her needs met. In the summer of 1973, John returned to live with me. We were living in a townhouse with other people. I loved the sun porch bedroom that we had. Everything was so beautiful—when it happened again. I just remember that everyone was trying to force me to eat and I did not even want to sit at the table. Imagine feeling like you have the flu and having people trying to force food down your throat. These were liberal days, so everyone was very tolerant of this thing and loving. Sometimes, people would refer to it as a breakdown; it never felt like a nervous breakdown to me. I was never nervous!

It felt like I had a bad case of the flu accompanied by suicidal thoughts in the down phase and complete and total physical pain. I always would get severe cramping in my legs, nausea and a feeling of fatigue unequaled by any other illness. It felt like I fell into a big black hole, never to be seen again.

This time I was emaciated and there was no relief in sight, when finally my parents stepped in and I went to a prestigious hospital in Southern New Jersey.

I always hated this hospital thing. After all, this thing felt so physical, but you are forced to hammer leather onto wood and do all these humiliating things during the recuperating process. I knew that none of these things really helped me to recover. Plus the humility of being strip searched. I was too feeble to commit suicide, now. Only time or some treatment could help!

After a few weeks, the doctor decided to try eight electric shock treatments on one side. Imagine all your life, your brain is the most important body part to you, and the doctor recommends eight shock treatments! You are hoping to become a college professor and bang—you are faced with getting electric shock treatments. I was scared to death again. What effect could this have on my cognitive ability? Will I remember anything about my past? Does the treatment really work? Am I going to look like my aunt with a dull gaze? All of this did not seem fair to me, but ultimately I took the treatments, wondering: Is this the end of a quality life for me? I was back to myself after eight treatments, with some earlier memories a little fuzzy. At first I woke up each morning from a false deep sleep to orange juice and a danish, wondering, "Who am I?" I had it explained to me again and again while I sat on the edge of a cot with a very nice psych nurse holding my hand. "Wake up, Salvina, it's all over." All I could remember was lying down on a cot and counting backwards, dropping into a deep, silent sleep. The doctor said that I should never again let it go so long without treatment. It only gets worse.

It is perfectly normal to be afraid of shock treatments. I have never seen anyone who was not scared before the first treatment. But with hindsight I know better. My cognitive abilities were unchanged after the treatments and I am perfectly able to enjoy every aspect of life. Now I know how unfair it was to vice presidential candidate Thomas Eagleton when he had to drop out of the race because he had had electric shock treatments. Here is where we need more education. People need to know more about mental illness. There is serious talk about keeping a record of those who seek treatment for a mental illness in a similar database as for criminal records. I fail to see the correlation. Mental illnesses do not necessarily translate into flaws. While a small part of mental patients may be violent, many others live with it and are successful professionals. If Winston Churchill could have untreated manic-depression and still do everything he did, why should treated people sometimes encounter discrimination? Was Handel in a hypomanic state when he wrote the Messiah? Probably, yes! Was Abraham Lincoln in a hypo-manic state during the Civil War? Only his severe periods of depression are documented, but his eloquence at other times in his life may be indicative of mild highs.

At least John did not back away; he came to the hospital a lot. He even moved with me near the hospital after it was all over. When I was released I was probably mildly high, not properly diagnosed and emaciated. I was ready to take on the world again! The doctor warned me against marrying John. I guess he saw in him what I did not want to admit. He seemed to feel that there were people around me that had a lot more problems than I had. I believe John really loved me, though.

I found a job at a local factory and John was not working. I had 12-hour shifts on a conveyor belt of dried chicken, looking for bones—not exactly the job I had aspired to earlier. I would come home, take a bath and feel like I was bathing in chicken soup. I love bubble baths, but this was absurd. However, that job helped me to retrieve my confidence, and for this I am grateful.

It took me a few months to be ready to face real life and work on finishing my degree. The university was very sophisticated about mental illness. My specific problem, however, had not yet been named. In those days it was almost a status symbol to have something like this because so many talented and famous people did. Only well-informed people understood that the problem was one of chemical imbalance.

My dad must have concluded that I was no longer a good investment, so he stopped paying for my tuition. He let me use stocks that my grandfather had left me to pay for school. His dream of me turning out to be an international lawyer was no longer possible. I was like a racehorse that broke a leg in mid-race. At least he didn't shoot me! I thought, but implicitly he did put me out to pasture. That hurt because I knew it was not necessary, and it certainly did not stop me.

John and I rented an apartment with friends in the city center. I was working part-time at a day care center and I was feeling relatively certain that "that thing" was behind me. I decided not to go to Taiwan for a year of study abroad. I was afraid of what would happen if I were overseas when "that thing" would hit again. I was afraid to let go of John. He was my long term flagpole during my illness, but somehow, I overlooked how irresponsible he could be. Why didn't I notice that I was the only one doing everything? Subconsciously this is probably why I kept putting off the wedding. After two years of living together, our parents were pushing. John came from a lovely family with whom I just became closer and closer.

Neither set of parents thought our marriage would last, and eventually they were right. They knew and I knew it could not last. I was far too consciencious and he was all too laid back. The day before the wedding Katherine sat with me on the beach and told me: "Salvina, you are making a big mistake. He is not right for you." Somewhere in my heart I knew that she was right, but I did not think anything could be done about it one night before the wedding. Little did I know that my husband to be was snorting cocaine with his friends the night before. Everyone was already here and everything was planned, starting with a sunrise service on the beach in the morning.

I wanted to run away again, far away!

CHAPTER 3

Tying the Knot so Smart

In June 1974, I married John in a lovely simple ceremony in the backyard of my parents' beach home. This was a civil wedding presided by a judge, to the great chagrin of both families. We wrote our own vows, something poetic, both modern and yet preserving the old tradition of breaking bread and sipping wine. We even silk-screened our own wedding invitations. I was creative enough to pull it off. I had beautiful bridesmaids in pink dresses and hats that were nearly flying off in the breeze. It was cool for that time of year. My father and mother walked me down the aisle and my father said, I "looked like such a beautiful woman" on that day. All the men wore big pink ties. After we were husband and wife, John's grandfather came up and gave me a big French kiss, and John said: "Oh, he is just welcoming you into the family, babe."

Grandma was our matriarch. One evening when I was at her house and the television announcer intoned, "It's ten o'clock. Do you know where your children are?" she answered with solid assurance, "I know where alla my children are alla the time!" And she did know where everybody was, even those in their fifties (not so old to me, now . . .) She was the family's pulse. Now she is gone. She held the family together as a whole unit. She was only recently described to me as the madonna of the household. We lived in that home for the first three years of my life and, which put a lot of pressure on mom; the expectations from her were high, but she lived up to them.

Everybody loved my grandma. There was nothing unlovable about her. Grandma put in a word for the bride's father's family, and I'll try to reproduce it: "Some people tink Siciliana dey d'woist kinda people, but I tinks dey d'best!" Cheers and clapping from our side. It was the boost my father's family needed because my husband's family was mostly of French descent with just a little Italian sprinkled in.

After the ceremony, dad came up to me and said that it was the most beautiful ceremony he had ever attended. Then he said to me as he always did: "Salvina, always remember that if things do not work out, you always have a roof over your head and three meals a day with me." He continued to provide a lot of security to us children. This would eventually turn out to be a promise he could not keep because he ultimately died.

John and I decided to spend our honeymoon in Vermont with my friend Carrie. She was always so pleasant to be with. During that visit, the illness hit me once again. I was walking along a path in Vermont, through fields that still had their golden evening light, past hills where I had skied, walked and collected wildflowers, and I was thinking about dying. I couldn't think about anything else.

Carrie's boyfriend, Jim, was also there. He is a psychologist. I thought, maybe I could walk back to Carrie and Jim's home and lie down in their guest bedroom and die. John, Carrie and Jim were a quarter-mile behind me, at the church supper, gobbling down fried chicken, corn and doughnuts. But their chatter pierced my ears; the smell of the food was nauseating; the last flare of the sunset blinded my eyes, always extra-light sensitive in the down phase. The sheer thought of all those human bodies was an intolerable burden. If anyone had even glanced in my direction, I might groan "Oh let me alone, please!" It was much better that I go.

My friends tell me that it is difficult to reach out to me in the down phase because I go into my own little fetal position and I do not want to talk to anyone. They remember seeing me in that non-communicative fetal position. I rarely want to talk during these times and I am in tremendous physical pain.

John turned to me when I started to walk away, and I'd shaken my head, warning him off. Just another "no," and he would have had enough of them on this honeymoon. Why did this have to happen on my honeymoon? Each night, I lay like a heap of stones on my side of the bed. I could not help it. There was no question of love, light or joy. I was beyond all that. There is no such thing as wanting anything romantic during an episode. I wanted to cry, but John would not let me. All I could mumble was, "Why me, why me, again?" and "I do not think I will ever get better."

From this perch, one cannot see a possible recovery.

I sincerely believed it would never happen again. I had become this pitiful creature in just one day. Just one week ago everything was normal as normal can be just before you get married, but the doctor at the hospital warned me that there was no guarantee that it would never happen again. Will my whole life be plagued by this on and off?

John, at least, was patient with me. He loved my thick curly brown hair, smooth silky skin, dimples and bouncy personality. In retrospect, I wonder if he did not know that I was his ticket to financial security.

I liked his athletic blondness, a way of walking as if he owned the world and, at the same time, a laid-back style. He was aristocratic in background and really smart. What a waste! We complemented each other well, at first. He could beat me at any word game. John still had a sixties point of view that carried over into the seventies and eighties. If it feels good, do it. We all need our space. He gave me a lot of freedom maybe because he needed a lot of freedom. At the time, it suited me fine. I realize now how bad he really was for someone with my illness. Security and structure are extremely important in the life of the bipolar.

I have found before someone starts to go into a mood swing, there is an initial uneasiness, a warning, a sense of something looming just below the horizon. All you want to do is run, hide, and make yourself invisible. But this is impossible, because the storm (or, shall we say, tornado) is already inside of you. Black clouds come whirling up, spreading and spreading until they cover your sky and throw your world into deepest shadows. Other people are mere ghosts and you are all alone. Nothing counts. There is no future to imagine. Nothing will ever improve unless you die.

No, I didn't try suicide, but as it happens in many cases, I have had suicidal thoughts. I simply stopped eating. I did not take care of myself. I couldn't care less. John did not attempt to entertain me out of it. He knew from the past that all we could do is wait for it to pass. He did remind me to drink my fortified milkshakes or mashed potatoes which was about all I could get down that might get some nourishment into my body.

It is not much fun, going on a honeymoon with a wife in that state. Depression is anything but romantic. In the extreme low, the libido all but disappears. Conversely, in the high, the libido is overactive. In the low, sounds can be amplified, piercing to my ears. I used to wear earplugs during these times.

Bipolar illness is a relatively recent diagnosis and it has a tendency be over diagnosed. Most people know that it has to do with a chemical imbalance in the brain, but they understand little else. It is almost fashionable, in some circles, to claim to have it; but in a real crisis situation people rarely know enough to help. It is not a pleasant situation. The patient behaves in ways that are considered unacceptable. Naturally, those who care about appearances have a hard time accepting that one of them is manic-depressive. My own family's initial reaction was denial. You cannot imagine the hurt caused by the inability of one's immediate family to empathize, or even by their inadequate attempts to understand. For years they "explained it away," as though it was not a real disease but a figment of my imagination. They never even referred to it with other medical concerns. They discussed dad's heart condition, my niece's illness, but my battle for my life was never mentioned. They couldn't see it for what it was. I had to survive, so I ignored them and fought valiantly to save my life. I realized that I would need to be strong and to educate myself.

Unlike my family, John was emotionally supportive and not afraid of my illness. That was different. From a different perspective, however, it played into his hands. Because I was afraid to leave him and handle it all on my own, he was being quietly kept. Even he did not understand or try to understand anything technical about the disorder. It was probably a combination of my family's attitude about my illness and the fear of being by myself with this, that made me move forward into a marital relationship that I knew was doomed to fail. In other ways, too, my life was lived according to the Taoist philosophy: just sort of falling into whatever came my way without much planning.

Here I was on my honeymoon and sick again. I did not want to believe that I had gotten eight shock treatments for nothing.

I was forced to believe it. By the time we visited our first set of friends on the honeymoon, I spent my time face down with a pillow over my head in bed. I was too fatigued to move. I heard my friends asking John: "What does she eat?" or "What can we do?"

He knew enough to simply answer, "Nothing, nothing. It is best just to leave her alone when she gets like this. It passes. You'll see."

"When?" they asked. "Whenever," he answered.

John was always good at reassuring me that this too will pass. I was always sure it would never pass! The good news is, this time it took only two-weeks. The bad news is, it was my two-week honeymoon. Neither of us enjoyed it very much, but we made the best of it.

By the time we arrived at Carrie and Jim's home, I was even worse. They kept making efforts, like the little church supper in the quaint little town; they thought this would surely cheer me up. When will people get it? Nothing but medication works on biological depression! There is a difference between clinical (behavioral) and biological depression. Nothing cheers you up in biological depression until a drug works.

I had come to certain conclusions early on that would later change, never to go the shock treatment road again. I developed distaste for a medical community that was not really helping me. Almost three years after my first episode I still had no tangible diagnosis. I also disliked hospitals and I wanted to avoid them as much as possible. They seemed to be set up for people with clinical problems, not for those with biological disorders. We are stuck with this set up until they reclassify this illness. My real treatment began when I encountered the specialists and research community of bipolar doctors. But one thing I knew, I could not let this thing run my life! I wanted a full life and I wanted to do whatever I could not to let it get in my way too much!

I'm a survivor!

CHAPTER 4

No Wonder Why I am Such a Character

From age nineteen to twenty-nine, the illness began to show a pattern and still went undiagnosed. Those are supposed to be the best years of a woman's life in terms of looks, desirability and self-confidence, or so I have been told. And precisely in those ten years, I had a tornado brewing inside me, the beginning of a roller coaster ride: three years in a mild high, which led me to believe that this was my well state. While in the mild high, I was very productive, very upbeat, very energetic and creative. To quote a friend: "You were always the life of the party." Everyone always invited me to their parties because without me, it might be lifeless. Why hire entertainment if Salvina was there doing great imitations and telling good and funny jokes?

Then came six months in severe depression . . . every three years that is. Depression would always start in October and end in March. I used to refer to October as Black October. Eventually I lost a husband, but I was finally diagnosed and treated. I sort of gained my family back. Over time, I rebuilt my professional credibility in the broadcasting ratings business. But when I went into a down, I finally knew I was sick.

There was a long swoop that took me into pain, dabbling in mysticism and eventually living like a Guinea pig in the country's most famous research hospital. I was desperate for a long-term answer. I was still in my early thirties. I could still recoup. Really, I was treated humanely by the research community and with respect and this is where I really learned about my disorder.

Black October, which invariably came around every three years, would still surprise me every time. Something dark would hang over me and the desire to escape mounted to terror. I felt that there was no exit, and then it came, submerging all my natural energy into deep depression. The depression lasted six months and changed me from a super-achiever who needed little sleep into someone that could barely force herself to get out of bed. I became a creepy invalid, drained of energy and convinced that I was dying of some treacherous disease. What did it matter that most of the time I was highly organized and motivated? When it hit, I could barely hold onto a thought, except the obsessive one that I was dying or wanted to die. I remember once, in college, going in and talking to a psychologist about all these symptoms. I shared with him a concern that raised as an observant Catholic perhaps God was punishing me for indulging in Chinese mystical practices. "Well, perhaps you have reached nirvana," he said.

If nirvana is reaching some kind of perfection, I knew for sure that I had not reached it. What I probably did reach was a bad, albeit funny, psychologist. This was no joking matter. I was suicidal. I was questioning God.

After graduation and marriage, I had to decide what to do with a degree in Chinese language. A recession hit shortly after I graduated and my college professor and friend discouraged me from pursuing academe. He said that track was getting more and more competitive and with the recession, it would not be practical to pursue a PhD in Chinese. He felt that the language departments would be reduced to native language teachers.

John had a lifelong dream to become a golf pro. There is a certain track for that, but at first track one makes next to nothing. I encouraged him to pursue his dream. He started in the golf business as an assistant pro and in order to get some money in the home, I took a menial job at a television ratings company while looking for employment in my field. In 1974, there were few opportunities for someone with just a BS degree in Chinese language. Like most graduates in Chinese, I was disappointed that no one offered me a position as ambassador to China at the age of twenty-one. The challenge of Chinese language intrigued me, and so much of the world's commerce seemed tied in with Asia and the countries of the Pacific Rim. How can I translate this into immediate cash, I kept asking myself?

I wrote President Jimmy Carter about the situation of underemployment in that economy and he responded by lining me up for an interview with the CIA as a translator. That did not match well with my liberal inclination at that time, but I did go to the interview so as not to be ungrateful. Now I would have loved to be proficient enough in the language to translate for an intelligence organization.

At the time I did not know then what a TV ratings company was about. In the broadcasting industry there is a high job turnover. I moved with the flow, all the way to New York, and each new move brought me together with a new home, a grocery store, new doctors and especially a new hairdresser. Finding a new hairdresser takes skill because that's the person with whom one shares everything. I remembered that in broadcasting "loose lips sink ships." You need someone who is excellent—television is visual, after all—and one who knows how to keep secrets. You have to talk to someone.

Dad must have hoped that I would marry well and be set for life. I married into a wonderful family, but my husband was not the best catch for financial security. Our group of friends was climbing past us on the economic ladder: a new car in the parking lot; a better job for someone else's husband; even a move to a little house in Virginia; none of this seemed to matter to John. For all his quick wit and intelligence, John was allergic to work with a livable income. All this time, I was developing a healthy appetite for responsibility. I had become a workaholic.

I am not the typical codependent. People like John hang around as long as you enable them. When you stop, they simply look for another enabler; they do not change. Yet, with all the aggravations, I did really love John. I wished we could have worked it out. He was so bright with so much potential. We even had a lot of good time together. We played golf together. Even though I was a hacker—and not a very good one—I always played with three other pros after hours for nine holes. If I slowed them down too much, I just picked up.

As a golf professional he had to listen to all the golf stories of all the members of the club. They did not reciprocate. So, after every tournament, he would come home and I would listen to every hole of the tournament shot by shot. It would go something like this:

"At the first hole, it was a par five, dogleg to the right, I took out my driver." I suppose you get the picture: the tournament shot by shot and hole by hole. If he had a 36-hole tournament, I would always ask if we could do the second eighteen the next night.

I cannot say that it was all bad. He was well liked. We did go to a lot of golf tournaments. My husband was a member of the US PGA and played on the local mid-Atlantic tour. We often walked the national tour events and I had the opportunity to meet some famous golf pros, but being around the rich and famous must have had little impact on me.

What was he planning to do with all his gifts and talents? I wondered. Nothing, I would later learn. I will either have to be the breadwinner in the family or get out. I am not a good partner for co-dependency. Half-and-half, OK; but co-dependency, no, thanks.

Shortly after I began to work in broadcasting, I was offered a professional position. I sat next to a girl named, Jean. She would play an important part later in my life and we are still very good friends. We were both initially overseers of interviewing field staff and I still did not fully understand what the company did. I was doing a pretty good job and I enjoyed the people I worked with. We needed a roof over our heads and food to eat. John did not seem to care that his assistant-golf-pro job was paying very little. It never increased much from there the whole time we were married. My salary, however, saw significant increases over time.

I was slowly growing in my field and becoming more and more professional and less and less idealistic. I was shedding my campus liberalism and taking on a conservative approach more suitable to the work force, more in keeping with my subdued preppy wardrobe. I only felt strange when I came home to our nice apartment in my pinstriped suits, high-necked career blouses and business heel pumps. I began to grasp what television ratings were about and was slowly working myself up the ladder. I also started graduate school at the same university; a Master's degree in demography would help me advance. I was focused on my job and school.

John, meanwhile, was getting nowhere fast. We were drifting apart. I did not want to go to the drug parties anymore and that led to hanky panky on his part. It hurt in a deep way, a way that is difficult to trust again, a way too deep to talk about.

The ratings company was also paying for my graduate education, not a small sum of money, a nice perk. Those were the days. Companies were like families and there was a certain amount of security one could depend on in exchange for loyalty. My good friend and golf buddy, Gloria, would always laugh: I was so bad with my woods that no matter how long the shot was from the tee, I would put my hand over my visor and say: "It looks like an eight iron to me." It became a joke between the two of us. Gloria grew up amidst tremendous wealth and fame. She has always been a special and loyal friend, in good times and in bad times. She was also loyal about visiting me at hospitals later. She liked my ability to keep a sense of humor amid the storm.

We frequented a racquetball club, too. John liked to play with my boss. We would all have such a good time. I was very competitive at this game. Perhaps being in that mild high between times of depression, meant the adrenaline unnaturally flowed through me, giving me the surges of energy that were really atypical. Luckily for me, there was nothing obviously wrong with me during these long time periods.

At one sales meeting, we had a dinner party at John's country club. That was some party! The VP of Sales, Andre, about whom I will say more about later, turned it into an open bar affair. The place was rocking and there was a lot of food. I remember that one local non-sales executive (who will remain unnamed) drove out of the club right over the eighteenth green. I do not think much work was done the next day. I do remember that my husband was leaving town for a tournament and when I was leaving I headed towards him to kiss him goodbye and I felt Andre staring at me. I wondered what he was thinking.

I had received more than one compliment by members of the sales force that I was strong in customer service. I knew almost everyone in the company. I was there for 6 years. Sometimes I wish I never left. There was a lot of work, but there was a lot of fun, too. We all spent time together outside of work. Perhaps that is what motivated us to work so hard during the sweeps and other crunch times.

But Black October was approaching. The third October came around again, and this time I felt the stirrings of a long change, not just a two-week lull and then back to normal. It happened on a weekend when I was scheduled to entertain interviewers for business. There I was forcing myself into work, forcing myself to do everything, forcing myself to just talk. I especially remember that I dreaded picking up the phone because the sound of a voice on the phone was piercing my ears.

Jean sat me aside to inform me that I was not caring for my personal hygiene enough, the way that I needed to. One could care less how one looks when one is down. I tried harder, but I knew it was not possible. She stood by me nonetheless. They did not understand, but no one was particularly judgmental. By March, I was back to my usual energetic and overly productive self, so, whatever it was, it was tolerated without question.

The first signs of trouble in my marriage were surfacing; it was clear, I was tired of paying all the bills, of keeping John financially. I was raised by an old country Italian father who provided for his family. A woman needs to feel secure.

I wanted separate bank accounts. "What did you say?" asked John. "I want separate bank accounts and we can both pay half the bills," I answered. "No," said John. "I do not want one of those marriages. It's our money. Come on babe," words that came to him easily and often, "You know we fit." He was a smooth talker. I have a name for that: a heel clicker. Andre was a heel clicker, too. I always fell for them or else for men who were really good at their work. Truthfully, John had a much better end of the deal and he was using my hard-earned money for his needs.

We were preparing to go to a friend's wedding. He was in the wedding party and I was not. During the reception, he left with the sister of the groom and re-emerged. I was mortified and made sure to let him know all the way home by hitting him with my purse. He retorted, "We just went out to get Lily's shoes."

Then, I received a letter from the girl apologizing for what happened. She said in the letter that she did not know that people believed in monogamous relationships anymore. I was even more livid that he not only committed adultery, but lied about it to me. There was nothing left for me inside.

Sometimes, I would go to Jean to talk about my marriage problems in private. She always took the conversation back to Jesus. I would just tell her that maybe that is the solution for a black woman from Mississippi, but not for me.

Things were deteriorating quickly from that point on. You have to be a victim of adultery before you can really understand how difficult it is to recover from it. There is an element of trust that can never be recovered. I was changing, he was constant. Mr. Peter Pan, we were drifting apart on a fast current, white water rafting to different destinations.

After a few years, I was promoted to the television products department where it was easier to get recognition and go somewhere. People there were less threatened by young people with ambition. In fact, it was appreciated and encouraged. I really started growing professionally and learning a lot here. Also, there was a group of us that were just like a family. We worked hard, but we also played hard. We rented cottages on the weekends, went on whitewater rafting trips, 30-mile bike rides along the canal in downtown and just fun times interspersed with hard work. I was moving up the ladder and the pay scale.

My company published the bible of the broadcasting industry, called "the book," which were quarterly market reports, grading local stations' performance for both radio and television. (I happened to work in television.) Whether the stations used our systems or the rival's, "the book" was required reading for all.

I bought new clothes, had wonderful vacations—company sponsored— where "the gang" brought sleeping bags and rented an A-frame house once, the better to enjoy the glories of red and gold autumn. When I was not in one of those horrendous swings, I loved the autumn. Yes, autumn, I counted them carefully and there was one secret I did not share with "the gang;" the secret about black October. I was even promoted within this department to work on a new system that outputs special reports. I'll never forget one client in particular from a New York firm that is no longer in business. He wanted his reports so quickly and we were not online then. I would need to drive them to the airport at night to get them into his hands by first thing in the morning.

Customer service was a lot better then than now. We really hopped to serve our clients. The sales team appreciated my understanding of the need for quick service and often asked me to New York to make presentations on the product with them. I was steadily gaining professional confidence.

There was always some chemistry between Andre and myself, maybe it was just another Frenchman. For those that have come out and asked and for those that did not have the nerve to ask: we never had an affair! Even in my liberal days, I did not believe in having affairs with married men. It is that loyalty thing of old. I have always put a great value on the sanctity of marriage. He would, however, play an important part of my life, later. He was silver-haired; he reminded me a bit of my adored father-in-law. The last time I'd seen him I was coming out of a mild depression and was decidedly frumpy. This time his eyes told me, I was a butterfly. Andre was married and I was married. Something tenuous hung in the air between us, unvoiced, but he watched me all evening. I was dancing at a business function and I loved dancing, then. We even danced to "New York, New York" that night. That is true in television, if you could make it in New York, you could make it anywhere. I did, despite my illness. I did make it in New York, for a while!

I returned to work from this gala event to find out that they wanted me to write a report on the marketability of the system I was working on, how much income it produced, etc. I had no idea at that moment I was writing a bit of a death sentence. The system would be buried, but no one talked about firing me. They would just find me another problem to solve. The only problem was, I also knew that that third Black October was at my doorstep again. I would have no control to stop it. I felt as though I was whispering to God: "Please do not mess with my brain again," but of course, that was useless. I had an idea: as long as the system I was working on would be shelved, I would take a leave of absence to work on my Master's degree and that way no one would know any different in the television department.

I left for one semester at school, not sure exactly how I would get through it. I did mostly, but it was difficult. The same way I took my undergraduate comprehensives, I got through it in a fog. In fact, once the top specialists got hold of me, they were amazed at how much I accomplished from a sick state. My company promised me a job would be waiting when I returned. They even dangled a promotion in front of me. It seemed I could not do anything wrong at that place as long as I got out in time, before I fell to pieces again. I said my good-byes with the knowledge that it was none too soon.

A loan for school did come through. The other little matter was how to handle full-time classes with my barometer down to zero. I decided to go to a doctor instead of psychologist this time and the doctor prescribed an antidepressant drug, a tricyclic, to be exact, and said: "You should be feeling better in about two weeks." Four days later, I had racing thoughts and I was so horny, I could barely control myself. I was pacing with no place to go. I was driving like a maniac. In fact, I was stopped for speeding and needed to show up in court. Fast driving is another symptom of the manic phase. I called my doctor about these symptoms. She said: "You are manic. Now we will know how to treat you, and your life should be much better, now."

This would prove to finally positively diagnose me as manic-depressive, or bipolar, whichever name you prefer. The drug itself induced a full-blown manic episode; this would only happen to someone with the disorder.

She pulled me into the hospital, put me on a takedown drug named Haldol. I was like a zombie for a few days and then she put me on the treating drug of choice, lithium. Instead of being reassured about this lithium thing, I was, frankly, scared. I am very sensitive to drugs and that haldol was enough to turn me into a zombie. Luckily, I had good doctors all along that protected my mind. But I was still anxious, thinking, "What does this mean for my life, my career? What am I going to be like after I am stabilized?"

I am a classic bipolar. I do not know how it was missed for so long. I also happen to be one of those bipolars for whom anti-depressants can be deadly. For me they both induced mania and sped up my cycle, and worse yet, they have been given to me over and over again. I am especially sensitive, remarkably sensitive, doctors would say.

Bipolars are usually the most interesting and creative people on hospital wards, generally professionals. From my experience, they tend to be very smart people. On this particular ward, there was a young girl who was psychotically high. She had gone off her medication. She thought, temporarily, that she was Princess Leia. She was also doing drawings of everyone on the ward and they were excellent. They restabilized her on medications and all was well

To make matters worse, John's latest mistress was taking my laundry to me in the hospital. "What do they think, I'm stupid?" I thought. Somehow I weathered through all of that and just kept on fighting for my life.

Hey, you can live with hypomania. It's a much milder version of the high phase of the disease. You are positive, optimistic, forceful and interested in everything. You will always get a job because whoever is hiring will see you as a real live wire. Hypomanics are people at the crest of their abilities; they get things done, they can work incessantly, sometimes obsessively. I'd apparently been living with a still milder phase of hypomania for years, juggling school, sports and jobs on little sleep. There's no pain, you feel good most of the time and, of course, you would never think to go to see a doctor. Well, that may have been one of my secrets of success, but my baseline is very energetic nonetheless, now known and documented by top treating doctors.

I returned to work, looking well and with every appearance of confidence. They said, "Welcome home" and "It does not matter at all," and offered me a choice of three jobs. The personnel department said that manic-depression was a controllable illness, no problem. I told them the truth. I did not still fully understand how dangerous it could be to tell people, to "come out", even your own family. People use it against you when they want to, in industry, in familial money matters, etc. I chose the television department with all my friends to reacquaint myself with life.

I had to show up at court about the speeding ticket I had gotten in a high phase. John and I walked into the courtroom and noticed that the judge was Italian. Well, I did have a note from my doctor, too, stating that this was a symptom of my illness. I got off with nothing. Good thing, because these tickets are expensive. I am sure the judge was suspicious about the claim that speeding is a symptom of an illness, but it is true. He probably thought, "What will they think of next."

I suppose my marriage was convenient for my immediate family as they chose not to come visit me during my hospitalization or otherwise. The choice was always to pretend that it did not exist at that time. It was too difficult to face.

Soon after coming out, I was back in the work routine. Nothing had changed in my home life, in my marriage, excepting the confidence of knowing my illness was controllable. My need to stay in the marriage was becoming less and less.

One night John did not come home until 3 a.m.; actually this was happening a lot. I drove up to the club and there he was hosting a party for teenagers by the pool. I knew then I could not stay with him. He could bring home any kind of disease. He was influencing teenagers the wrong way. I could not be a part of this. I had to think the unthinkable. That night when he arrived home, I made it clear that he would be sleeping downstairs and we would be talking in the morning.

We talked in the morning. I think he was shocked that I was finally prepared to act on what we had talked about. He did not have the money to move out, so he stayed with me for another six months, sleeping downstairs. Maybe we both knew that despite our differences, the initial relationship was based on love and we both needed some time to adjust to the decision. Besides, I was really close to his family and that would prove to be an even greater loss to me. You see, though, I was told that my life was permanently changed and I was well, so I did not even consider a future with these same problems. In a sense I may have used him too, for emotional support. There are always two sides to a story. I know he felt I worked too hard and too long. I was selfish to keep him around because of my illness.

Once the preliminaries for the divorce began, he was casual again. "You'll find someone else. I've noticed that several men have eyes for you," John said. I have not up until now. He was right, but I never acted on it. I was faithful to John, as difficult as that was. The high level men in television are polished and that in its way was heartbreaking.

Some part of me mourned over the end of my marriage; I felt halved. We were together for ten years. I do not believe in divorce now, but I know from my experience that divorce is another one of those experiences that leaves anyone— bipolar or not—in a temporary state of grief. I found a place to live in a house where young professional people live together. I biked with friends along the Potomac, and I began to date again. It is important for a recently divorced woman to feel that she is still lovable.

It was a good year for young attorneys in their Washingtonian yuppie uniforms. I was living, as I loved, within the District of Columbia. I reverse commuted from the city. I love the city. I had a real sense of loss about my in-laws, but I felt a sense of relief regarding my ex-husband, like a big weight was lifted off my shoulders. He seemed almost oblivious to how much of a burden he really was to me. I had no idea how much of my salary was being drained just by our marriage until afterwards. I had no idea how much his affairs and late nights drained me physically. I really felt a sense of lightheartedness and relief for the first time in years. I knew I did the right thing for my health and for my pocketbook. His father always said that he could have helped me with this illness had John provided the right security and structure for me. His father was a fine medical doctor and they were fun to be around. It turned out we had similar personalities in the end . . . a shock to John.

I met a nice man at the evening song service on Palm Sunday at the Washington Cathedral. We started to see one another. We went to the very best restaurants in town and also had bread, wine, grapes and cheese picnics in the parks, as we read poetry. He soon wanted a commitment, and I was only months out of a failed marriage. The echo of his, "I do not want you to date anyone else!" scared me. I stopped seeing him, too. Sometimes, I wonder if that was a mistake.

I was sent to Chicago frequently for work and I would work a twelve-hour day and then go down to South Chicago to listen to a blues band until the early morning. I cannot believe just how much I accomplished without getting sick . . . or maybe I was a little sick. I liked jazz, classical and the blues back then, but especially the blues. I sometimes went to the French Quarter of New Orleans, the jazz capital of the world to me. I have always loved music, but my taste changed over the years.

At work, I was playing "follow the leader" with my friend Elizabeth, stepping into assignments she had just left while her chair was still warm. Elizabeth also went to the same university and she graduated one year ahead of me.

Now Elizabeth had come back from several years as Research Director at a major network flagship station. It had given her a status and a paycheck that frankly, I envied. My company was good to me and I had no intention of leaving it forever, but I wanted to increase my value to the company. Working directly in the field of network television would be exciting. Three years in and out of hospitals was not in my program. Elizabeth gave me a good reference.

I went down for an interview and got the job. Who could resist such an opportunity? After all, I thought I was medically better, too. My friends at work gave me a going away survival package present which included: a plastic machine gun, a little plastic tank, a bikini set, some Bromo-Seltzer and that is only what I remember. I knew they were trying to suggest I reconsider, and they, knowing me, knew it was like "talking to the wall". They took me to lunch at Chuck E Cheese, another poke at my good-sport and class-clown personality.

Of course, I had no idea that I was not yet stabilized. I suspect my confidence in leaving John was, at least, somewhat based on newfound wellness. I drove without stopping to my new destination in my recently purchased car. I bought it before I got the job in a hot climate and it had no air conditioning. I figured I would suffer plenty in the summer months. One of the station's employees found me a nice apartment. Later, I found out she really wanted my position. I guess I should be happy that she did not poison the place. It is such a competitive field and she really was not old enough or weathered enough for the job, yet. We eventually grew to be friends. Jane, however, helped to initiate me and then left to go to the sales department. I was on my own to find an assistant for the research department. I was now the Director of Research and Sales Development for the station. I reported directly to the sales manager of the station. He was in his early fifties and reminded me of my dad. That seemed old to me back then. Now, it is young, so very young!

I suppose Jane was suffering from what I had experienced, in needing to be appointed Ambassador to China, too soon. Amazing how we do not appreciate experience when we are young. Sadly, young people today are replacing experience to protect the bottom-line, but what about the quality of the work? She wanted my job, but she had to learn to accommodate.

I liked Tony a lot and he liked me. He was the Italian protective boss that reminded me of my dad. Despite being a female that was "making it" in the career world, something inside me always yearned to be protected by a man and the kind of protection dad had given me. It is still there, a deep yearning for that paternal security, financially and otherwise.

I reported to the station in my usual preppie uniform, which we all wore in Washington then; lots of pin stripes and buttoned up silk blouses. I dressed very feminine, but very professional. I was entirely unprepared for a room full of women wearing bright colors, flowing dresses and one thing that stuck out in my mind: more makeup. I was concerned about fitting in here. It was not only that our styles seemed mutually incompatible, I knew nothing about the certainty of my new job now. Only weeks after I arrived, the owner of our parent company died. What timing!

When an owner dies, the station is usually sold. A new management team comes in and you are out the door. The people who were checking me out as to what I was all about were all waiting for the ax to fall, hoping to survive the inevitable shakeup of personnel, and here I was newly hired and relocated to boot. Luckily, the staff at WTVJ could not see my knees shaking. "Last hired, first fired," I thought, "Is a rule with very few exceptions." Of course, politics comes into play, too.

"Good morning," I said to the room at large, noticing a few men in reassuring navy jackets. There were murmurs of a greeting. I guess everyone was waiting to see how I did before they showed any enthusiasm.

I was a skillful and ethical researcher and no games or hypes were likely to come out with my name on them. This did cause some contention with the sales department. "Sorry guys," I am just doing my job.

One of my functions was to put an estimate on specials coming down from the network and this would set the rate for advertising. I received one special and it was about the life of a fairly obscure prizefighter. When this special came down from the network, the sales department wanted me to set the estimate to the first airing of "Rocky." Do you know how ridiculous that request was? The sales department and I went back and forth over this one. We finally reached a compromise that I could live with my name on it. The made-for-television movie did not even perform to half of "Rocky". You see fellows, I did know something about ratings after all. Tony would forever try to intervene in these disagreements between sales and myself, but it was difficult. After all, he was like gombada, (godfather) to me. He treated me like a lady and he saw to it that I was treated like a lady.

I had traveled several hundred miles for my new job, sending the moving van ahead, a one-woman caravan. In that hot Chevy, I traveled into a climate with an affinity to Hades. The sun was so bright that it made one grateful for the shade of telephone poles, and the place was so flat that it made mountains out of speed bumps. There were flying super-bugs who shall certainly inherit the earth in tribulation time; and the green salamanders that kept climbing out of my bathtub drain! I called home to find out how to get this creature out of my tub. Whatever could hiss, crawl or fly welcomed me to my new home!

The station was housed in what had once been a movie theater. Inside, it was a labyrinth of doors, oddly shaped rooms and unexpected steps. Our parking lot seemed under siege; its high, protective fencing preserved our cars from the nearby ghetto where buildings were burned and damaged by riots.

I lived a successful, but often-lonely life. There was a small café nearby for breakfast or lunch. A Ma and Pa coffee shop tucked into the station's building. People from the newsroom were always there. It was the place to catch up on the latest news before it even went out to the public.

Everyone was transfixed the day Grenada was invaded by our troops. The news crew busting to get a first, like any news crew, ordered one hundred ham and cheese sandwiches to go!

I remember the day that Jessica Savitch died in an automobile crash. I arrived at the station early and went in to have breakfast. I was one of the first to know. There was all kind of rumors about what caused this accident, inside television. I thought, let the dead rest in peace! After reading the biography of Jessica Savitch, I learned that her dad was also a garment manufacturer. I could identify with her upbringing and what made her push herself, probably, into an early grave. I was sad that day for her; maybe I related to that need to drive and then drive some more. I have to do it! I cannot let them down.

Another morning, a story came in and they canned it. Suicide is not a story, but murder is. Millions of no names going to their graves with this illness with some cover-up story from embarrassment and stigma. That hit me hard that we have no voice. Our millions of deaths are not newsworthy.

I would always tease the weathermen at the station that they were the only ones who could be consistently wrong and still keep their jobs. As usual, I was working twelve-hour days and for the most part doing well at it. The most powerful man at the station liked me a lot. I knew I was safe as long as he was there.

Stations, at that time, subscribed to both my former company and the rival. Rich loved the management at my former company so he was happy to have a former employee on board the boat; unfortunately it was a boat headed for the fate of the Titanic.

He was equally happy to have a "research purist" as opposed to a numbers gymnast on board. He respected good research and statistically reliable results.

My day began at 7 a.m., usually, at the printer, getting off the ratings from the previous night, and distributing them throughout the station. Then, I would visit the human printers to see if any of my sales pieces were ready for distribution. The salespeople really needed these pieces with regularity and with speed. It was sometimes difficult to communicate this to the printers. A lot of people seemed to operate on a slower speed here than up north.

There were eight salespeople at the station. After just a few months on the job, I was summoned into Rich's office. His office was a little intimidating, done in airy blue and shining silver; it felt as though I was stepping into a cloud. Along the wall were five TV monitors, and I had to share Rich's attention with them as he clicked from one station to another. He was actually much less fearsome than that description sounds: a sandy—haired, pleasant-looking man in his sixties. He was a smooth executive who guided through a little social chitchat about his broadcasting background and then complimented me on one of my pieces that he had recently seen. I had caught his interest and respect and with a man like Rich, with a legendary reputation in broadcasting, that was rare. Sometimes, I feel that had I landed there earlier and younger, I would really "have made it" there. That was my real debut at the station.

Soon after, I was called into Tony's office. I'd seen him almost daily at meetings, but never alone. Now he really reminded me of my dad, garrulous, friendly, but at the same time tough. He was a type A, personality like myself. In his eyes you were either a lady or a slut. Luckily, I fell into the lady category. I knew how to talk to him, I had years of practice growing up. He said: "And by the way, Rich thinks you are a very smart girl."

I guess that is why I am suddenly in the inner circle. Rich likes you here. Frankly, no one else has to like you. There were moments that it felt like that. I put on a modest smile and then he added: "We'll work with you or work you to death, according to your point of view."

They bought me what was then a super computer with great expectations. I was so often distracted by Rich that I was not as attentive enough to sales, I think. I probably should have been. I was strong in research. I answered: "I'm looking forward to it."

I did work very hard at the station, seven-day weeks, twelve-hour days, sometimes. This was the usual work schedule for me in this job and others. I often visited my mom at the beach house for one week's vacation. I was called from morning until night in almost every television job. She would say: "Can't they leave you alone for one week?" I know an executive that was called while she was in the delivery room. It is that kind of industry.

Tony took me to lunch that day and it was great fun. He always took me out to the best restaurants. The expense accounts back then were a lot bigger than they are today. All the waiters knew and respected Tony and his expense account. We were like old friends by the end of the meal and neither of us were working at it. It was one of those natural friendships. He was the closest to family for me there.

These two men would become my mentors at the station and I learned a lot from them. Sometimes, I wonder if they are alive today. Tony was a character. One day I went into his office to ask a question and he motioned to me to be quiet and then used a motion as though he was reeling in a fish. I supposed that meant he was closing a deal.

By 9 a.m., when most of the local businessmen were just rolling up to their parking spaces, we were deep into sales meetings with the national and local sales managers. My immediate boss, the General Sales Manager, Tony, presided. Power plays went on all week, as the staff expertly dissected reputations and who was doing what to whom, but I minded my own business and spent a lot of time on the phone.

This was the usual routine during ratings "sweep" months or right after the quarterly book came out. I was working seven days a week, non-stop. I had no time to worry about power plays, if I would keep my job or if I would ever be sick again. The management still did not mention the word "reorganization," though the owner had been dead for months. They let us stew in our own juicy rumors that we were sold and we were not sold; the station would still be under the same management, so we were led to believe, and then "no," it would not. Heads would roll and then no, no, everything would remain as it is now. We were mostly told that everything would remain status quo. After all, they did not want everyone jumping ship.

I was getting external feedback that I had evolved into one of the top five affiliate local station research managers in the country, out of 214 markets. I believe that was one of my top accomplishments. I was being noticed externally, as well. I know one thing, Andre, who was trying to sell us the meters system, was becoming closer and closer to me. We often had dinners together with Tony and his wife, Katy, after meetings at the station. I had to monitor the progress of these meters because we had to make a decision between companies. At one million dollars per annum, a local market station could no longer subscribe to both services. This would eventually be the demise of my former company for television local market services. Andre was the only one who, in retrospect, had my best interest at heart. He repeatedly called me and said:

"Salvina, things are really going to come down there. You are well respected. Get out now. You have to think about number one, you know."

"Andre, I am safe as long as Rich is safe," I responded. Andre retorted, "Salvina, like I said, things are really going to come down there." Andre was right. As usual, I did not listen to good advice. I could not imagine it was going to be that big, but it was.

When Rich was promoted to the Corporate VP of all stations, a new face appeared from another station, Morton. Morton was a sweet-natured Southern gentleman that had temporary written all over his face. I did not have that much contact with him. Rich and Tony were my two main contacts. Tony had an internal enemy and his main goal was to have the research department report to him.

Therefore, I would often be in the middle of his target practice. Morton very nicely guaranteed me that this man was notorious for this kind of stuff, so just turn the other cheek.

This was my first experience, though, at watching certain people literally spending more time trying to figure out how to get someone in trouble or to lose their job than just working and doing their job. It is true that this industry has those that are cut throat as part of it.

During management meetings, Rich would walk around the room and ask everyone what they would do to solve a certain problem. When he came to me, I said mine and he invariably would say, "That's what I would do." That became an order from Rich and not an opinion. It meant . . .

"Team, get yourselves moving on this one."

Rich was grooming me for VP corporate research. I thought I was going to make it after all. I would have excelled within that scenario. I guess there is a lot of naivety in me, too; naïve for calling the power plays in advance.

I came to be known as his right-hand lady, a protégée of sorts. We had an uncanny way of looking at things the same way for business. We did sign the first meters contract in the market and some people were very upset about it. We did become the first local market to subscribe to meters; it was a better way to measure household data, albeit far more expensive. Surveys are becoming more and more difficult to conduct with accuracy. I was a perfectionist at my work.

At the time of the reorganization, I wish I had a paper shredder. Once Rich told me the outcome and I had to find the research to support it. That is putting the cart before the horse. There was one report I really wished I could have destroyed.

I would be kidding myself to deny there was a lot of Daddy's girl in these relationships. My mentors were old enough to have daughters my age, one did and she sounded as though she made as practical life decisions as I did. They may have been disposed to view me that way, but there was nothing cute about it. I think the relationships were also based on professional competence and mutual respect. Does that sound arrogant? I still believe it. But I had to push down the impulse to be candid with these friendly bosses about my illness; that would not be businesslike and could cost me my job, which was all I had left.

Strange, if you have a heart problem or diabetes, everyone knows why you curtail your diet and they will not force you to do something that will harm you. If you are a recovering alcoholic, they will gladly serve you ginger ale. However, if you have a physical illness located in the brain, people can run a mile. Hide the knives and scissors, here comes the nut. I had to keep this secret to myself. It is getting much much better now.

The station manager, who was really after Tony, now played a little trick on me one day. Every survey, we get advance ratings from a survey company. I always had a good relationship with my former company and I got them early. For one survey, however, I was out of the station at a seminar. This turkey called the survey company and told them I was not there to get the ratings, so to give the ratings to him. It was not even in his jurisdiction. Then he went into a staff meeting and announced that because I was not there to get the ratings, that my former company called him with the advance ratings. This is snake behavior to me. Morton told me not to pay him any mind because he does it to everyone. It was all about territory. I wondered how he had time to get all his work done while he plotted against everyone at the station.

My first inkling of what my hormones were getting ready to do to me happened after the station was already sold. We knew that much, but not the identity of the new owners. I didn't listen to the gossip and took only casual notice of the long black limousine which appeared, generally on Wednesdays. We came to refer to that as Black Wednesday at the station. Whose turn is it this time? Easy for me to figure out that I would be number four. Rich called me into his office and introduced me to this man. This man was, in my opinion, gorgeous. He was a handsome young man, a sharp dresser and represented some major broadcasting group on the West Coast. Wow, what a hunk. He was also Sicilian, on his father's side. I never met such a good-looking man.

Insomnia was only one of the symptoms I was developing. I was supposed to be well now, on lithium. I stayed on my medications. This did not feel like a depression or a full blown high, but it did feel like non-stabilized manic-depression. My libido was out of control. I was not sure I could keep it in control. I was going to the station earlier and earlier to work! Gradually, the signs of profound change in my biochemistry was making themselves apparent. At night, I would rush out on the streets, jogging for blocks and going nowhere. I would go into a bar and there is an air about a manic, a sexy, energetic air that captivates any possible recipient, really uncharacteristic behavior. I often twitched when I sat and I was driving like I was high again. This was higher than my usual high. I could usually exercise more control.

Then one day, I was sent up to my former company for a short business trip. I think, in retrospect, Rich knew this was the day that the ax would fall. He wanted me to be home with friends at my former company when I heard the news. In the early afternoon, that word came by telephone. Rich was asked to empty his desk and leave the station and a local general manager from the station across the street was now in charge. He was bringing his team with him. This was unprecedented in broadcasting history.

Andre called right after the news broke and I said, "My behind is grass, Andre! You were right!" Andre said, "Yes. Look for a job, now!" "They didn't even give Rich a gold watch after all those years in broadcasting. It's a tough business," I complained. "You are right, Salvina," Andre answered.

I could not tell Andre that I was too sick to look for a job. He would wonder what I was sick with. That would be professional suicide. Everyone equates this with stress, but that is simply not the case. I visited the doctor who had diagnosed me and had blood drawn and the response never varied, "Your lithium level is fine."

I returned to the station knowing that I was both a short timer and sick, no matter what my blood level said. I remember receiving a call from Elizabeth to find out how things were going in this mess and I just answered, "Om, Om! Just like Teng Xiao Ping, I am not passing re-education camp, Elizabeth!"

She laughed.

It is a good thing that I had developed a good close friend in Shannon, too, at the station. She really helped to see me through this time period. She was in the promotion department and creative. She had an artistic look, not like a gypsy, but running to reds and blues and chunky jewelry with big wooden beads. All that flamboyance was topped by a rosy, farm country face and blond hair. Her clothes mystified me. I had relaxed enough after nearly a year in this flamboyant town to wear turquoise, open-collared blouses with my preppie pearls and suit skirts. Shannon, on the other hand, was an extravagance of color.

We toured major craft fairs together and I found a different city with Shannon. We went out to eat sushi a lot and then we'd wrap it up with some pastries. I had very little appetite so Shannon would ask, "Are you just going to sit there and watch me pig out again?" I guess the "yes" is the best I could come up with.

When I think of Shannon, I remember laughter and word games that cracked us up. Shannon asked me, "What kind of a husband do you want the second time around, Salvina?" I answered, "I once told my ex-father-in-law that I wanted someone like him, but younger. I think the 'but younger' offended him. I am attracted to brains more than anything else. I want someone who is responsible, too. That would make up for my last husband. He will not dress as funny as you, Shannon. You know I still have that preppy lacy look to my suits!" "Yes, I know, square!" Shannon retorted.

I was determined not to leave the station until Tony took the ax. After all, they were my mentors. It was not always easy because the new management was trying to wear me down and make me leave.

They would constantly put my mentors down and I would always say, "I didn't see them that way." I always defended them during this reorganization and it was difficult.

Of all the people I knew, I had the strongest desire to share my secret with Shannon, but I was even concerned about her reaction. Shannon and I went to psychic fairs and we often got readings. They were not cheap. In retrospect, what a waste of money, but I was scared and they made me look forward to the future. I think my loyalty really hurt me in that situation. I cannot easily switch and pitch when you treat me well. Shannon, I suppose you could say, introduced me to my next spiritual phase, the New Age Movement. Television is full of it, starting with Shirley MacLaine on down. Anyway, it was easy to get hooked when your future hung with such fragility as mine at the time.

Depression was something that could be brushed off lightly and people would say, "Oh, I never get depressed." That would make me grit my teeth and turn away, knowing that they had no idea of what I meant. As for "manic," they heard "Maniac." They immediately wanted to protect their children from me and they became scared of me. Your typical manic is usually very motivated, and often supremely hard at work. A manic phase is like a wild explosion of energy, enthusiasm, super-creativity and incredible stamina. Hypomanics compose great plays, symphonies, write epic poems, make great fortunes if it only would go on at a certain level, but then you spin out of control, you lose all sense of good judgment and it becomes scary for you and others. In a wave of indiscriminate enthusiasm, you can spend the fortune, you can even uncharacteristically have an affair.

A stabilized bipolar does not get sick often, but when we do cycle into the high, we might need help. Sometimes, we need outside intervention to get us help, even when we are saying, "I'm fine!" Yet this miserable, grandiloquent disease brings out the best in some of its victims. Winston Churchill guided England to victory with his unmatched powers of inspiration. The bipolars I met during my hospital stays included lawyers, doctors, judges, bankers and educators, the brightest in our society. I went back to my university for my ten-year reunion in the middle of that mess at the TV station. Andre did not understand why I was not busy looking for a job. I asked Jean if I could stay at her home for the week. She said "fine." Well, the reunion went fine and it was time for me to return to work. It had been great to see old friends and party with them. Who was doing what and this time I was successful and looking well!

Then on Sunday morning Jean asked me to go to church with her and her family. I said "No way, thanks again. I will not go into a church!" I declined. She retorted, "Then stay home by yourself." I agreed to go to the service; I figured it could not hurt. I was sufficiently stubborn.

It was a small all-black church in the inner city of Washington, DC. The gospel music was great, so I guess I relaxed. I gave my heart to Jesus on that day and that would change my life forever. That was June 10, 1984. It changed my life from the inside out.

I returned to the station filled with peace, knowing that I was going down to get fired. My father said, "Go down and take it like a Cappello." He was tough. I was softer than he gave me credit for or maybe even knew.

One day my assistant Candy came in and said, "I cannot stand to see what they are doing to you here." I knew that Candy loved living there and could survive this thing. I had to cut the umbilical cord for her sake. I said, "You like it here. I do not. If you care about your career in broadcasting, get back in your office and start taking orders from Lynn, now. She is the new research manager."

I was there only in body. That was probably my most difficult task during the reorganization. I had to do it for her. She did really well after I was out of there. She became one of the best local market television media researchers in the country, even a network wanted to hire her. I felt cold at the time, but I did it for her own good. I was too attached to the old management team. There was no way I could survive this. Tony was finally fired. He left graciously and I submitted my resignation. I felt inside that I was too sick to work and with no one to believe me, since my lithium levels were supposedly normal.

As for me, I knew that this Lynn did not like me at all and there was mutual disrespect about that. I hoped to get out of there soon. My meetings with her were grueling. She kept telling me she was made an offer she could not refuse. Everyday was a nightmare to get through. Some people felt I allowed myself to be humiliated by staying, but I was loyal to my mentors as usual.

Andre called me and said, "Just remember adversity builds character, Salvina." I replied, "No wonder I am such a character, Andre"! Andre laughed.

I packed everything up. I drove nearly non-stop to my parents' beach house, always my refuge in times of trouble. It remains my refuge. I think it is my sense of humor through all of this that made me keep a handful of good friends standing by me when I arrived for another crisis or encounter with my illness.

CHAPTER 5

Walking Time Bomb

I made it home in record time, a sign perhaps that I was somewhat high. On the other hand, I just wanted to sleep in the hammock at my family's beach home. My mother's denial came shining through: "Well, you have been through a lot, dear. You are probably burned out." No way, I am always ready to work, so something was very wrong. All my friends were staying away. I suppose I was putting them off with high symptoms. The high really makes people run just when you need them to help the most. Besides, television executives are made of tough stuff.

All of my possessions were put into my parents' basement and once again my life was on hold for the moment. It seems that I would be exiled more than once due to this illness. I guess life could be worse. The island is a beautiful place where upscale people gather to beach. If you must be exiled, this is just fine.

A long time was about to begin where only a nurse's reading the Bible to me could comfort me while I waited for my drug trials to begin. I think, perhaps in this state, I made a few passes at Andre and he had backed off, as a friend, not entirely sure what was going on with me. Actually, from a well state he had made a few advances towards me, in the past. However, this was different. In his eyes, he was supposed to make the passes. Andre did not put this one in a box. He always said that I was always so appropriate in dress and demeanor. A high person is anything but appropriate.

Maybe some other friends just attributed it to the major loss, after all I was being groomed to be the VP of Research for all stations. Maybe I was having a so-called "nervous breakdown." From early July until September, I just secluded myself at the beach home, except for two occasions.

One brother was getting married in August that summer. I was the only sister not in the bridal party. I guess it hurt a bit, but I was always thought of as the "crazy" sister. I've yet to be allowed to baby-sit or have some special role with a niece or nephew. It seems that way to me anyway.

I went to the wedding dressed like any high woman would dress. Anyone that knew my conservative style of dress would have caught on to the fact that something was wrong with me. I wore this shiny magenta flimsy top with an off-white skirt. I thought I looked great, at the time, but I was actually sleezy. Perhaps that is why the photographer lopped me off the end of the family picture. Why didn't someone pick up that I needed the help of a high-level specialist in order to be well? I guess everyone lives in their own little world. Sleezy dressing is a symptom of the high phase, especially for someone who is not usually sleezy. By the way, you think you look great! There is such a lack of judgment in the high phase.

I did not feel high and I did not feel low, but I knew it was manic-depression again. I later came to find out that this is called a "mixed state," some elements of both states. It feels really uncomfortable from the inside. One feels completely disoriented from this state and yet one appears fairly normal in observation from the outside.

Well, my brother and his wife were off for their honeymoon and upon their return, my dad had a massive heart attack, at only 59 years old. He had to be revived a few times in the ambulance. It seemed his aorta was 90 percent blocked. He was in CCU for four days total. I was crying, but talking him through this. The doctors kept coming out of the room and saying, "Well, he is a fighter." We knew that interpreted into: "he is not likely to make it, but if anyone would, he would."

How much I worried about losing my dad. He was my pillar of strength. So strange that he would be struck so young. So strange that he was struck when I needed him so much.

My mother was supposed to go to Anchorage to help my sister with the delivery of her third child. I was chosen to be the surrogate grandma and go help my sister in Anchorage, Alaska. I did not know how much help I would be in my current state, but I took off. We had a terrible flight and were even caught in a down draft on the way down.

Well, my sister was overdue when I arrived, but that didn't stop her from taking me all around., The scenery was breath-taking. I was concerned about having to deliver a baby unprepared. My sister surely would have been a pioneer on the wagon train had she lived at that time. Now, keep in mind that I have an illness of the biological clock. Time zone changes should be made carefully and slowly and I just zipped to the West Coast in an already non-stabilized state. I can imagine that this just aggravated my already ill state.

We took daily trips a good ways from the city, and visited glorified nature. My sister, like my dad, loves nature. It came time for her to deliver and she and her husband went off to some natural birthing center. She was in labor for so long that the birthing center sent her to a hospital. Stubborn as she is, she arrived home late at night telling her husband, "If I cannot have a natural childbirth at the birthing center, I'll just have to have it here." Now I was really getting nervous about having to deliver a baby. I reminded her of Gone with the

Wind and Miss Scarlett and Prissy, "I don't know nothing about birthing babies, Miss Scarlett." Her husband finally talked her into going to the hospital to deliver the baby. They had a beautiful baby girl, who is 21 years old now. She is still beautiful with a delightful personality to go along with it.

This was a special experience for me, always working and never sharing special life events. My new niece added something a little special to the two boys already in the family. All of my sister's children are good children. She was the one person in my family that has always tried to understand and to stand by me. I talk to this sister nearly every night and she has given me a lot of emotional support during my illness. She always made me feel like a whole person. She never depersonalized me and she always tried to get me the help I needed. It is obvious when I become ill. Some people still choose to ignore it—and me.

When I arrived home, my sister was desperately trying to tell my mom, "There is definitely something wrong with her, she really needs help!" However, it fell on deaf ears as usual. That reaction from my family is more the norm than the exception. Hopefully, this will change with time. It is already beginning to change for the better. Sometimes I felt as though my family valued me less than a domesticated animal. They simply did not have the capacity to understand that mine was as real as any other physical disease. I returned home to no help. I had called the research manager at a station in the closest market to me and asked about job opportunities in that market. She indicated that research positions never open up in that market. I said, "Okay." And then she said, "Why don't you send in your resume anyway." I did. Within a week, I was called in to interview for a station across the street. Their research manager was leaving unexpectedly, with her husband. I was clawing my way out of the closet to be treated for a quality life.

By now, it was well into autumn and, in my opinion, too cold to be on the beach. I was just sleeping in my room at my parents' home further north and not doing much else when I learned about this job at a network affiliate, that would be considered a promotion from my previous job. I applied and got the job in a week. The only problem was, how was I going to work in this condition? My main goal was to get the attention of good medical help, which was impossible from my current perch and with the resistance of my parents. Like my dad, even with an illness like this, I am a survivor.

I wanted to beat "this thing." If I stayed at my parents' home, I would live in a closet like my aunt and be treated like an object; that was all my family knew about how to handle such things in those days. I was fighting for a normal and full life and I was fighting alone. You cannot talk about it, it can only be ignored. This did not seem fair to me. I did not go off my medications and I was still sick. This lithium was supposed to change my life forever!

I immediately contacted the nearest and best hospital and asked for a bipolar specialist. I was given the name of Dr. S and he was my first of several encounters with doctors that really understand this disorder and are exceptionally devoted to their jobs and patients. They are the research doctors. At first we hoped together to get me stabilized quickly and back at the television station working. Dr. S could see that I faced an uphill battle with everyone around me refusing to understand that this is a real illness. He told my father, "This is no different than your heart condition, but it is located in her brain." When he spoke with my mom, Dr. S just turned around to me and said, "They do not understand this illness."

It is as much a fault of the system because it should have been taken out of the mental illness status a long time ago, but there are politics involved since only psychiatrists are trained to treat it. This is more an illness of a hormonal imbalance of the brain than emotions. But the problem was that it is still placed in the category of a mental illness and that was not acceptable to them or anyone. Imagine having an illness like this and receiving such rejection from your own family because of their embarrassment. One is not only struggling to survive, but struggling with the stigma as well. Most of us encounter this stigma after treatment. Hopefully, it will continue to change in the near future. I repeat, it is getting much better and I expect it to get much better in the future.

Well, I was still showing up at the station every day and hoping to salvage both my health and my job. Every day it was getting more and more difficult to do. Then I developed suicidal thoughts as I was not becoming better. Dr. S could not check me into the hospital. I had no insurance. My mom and dad came to visit and were telling me that I would never work in my field again if I went into the hospital. I knew I probably would not live much longer if I did not receive treatment. I wanted treatment; I still back treatment. My parents were right about the general opinion of the public. You are less than yourself, you become stigmatized with treatment, but what becomes of you without it? It is still a tough call, but I needed help.

My parents tried everything, "We'll buy you a condo if you just keep working and do not go into the hospital." That is no different than telling someone with cancer, "We'll buy you a new car if you just do not take chemotherapy." Dr. S was upset with my parents and said they were not allowed to visit. He viewed me as being in a critical condition of bipolar disorder and he saw them as being completely non-supportive and not willing to become educated.

They were not alone. The stigma sometimes causes families to not want to listen. Other families really want to learn. People need to learn because this illness kills and I am only alive thanks to the perseverance of some very dedicated research doctors, and the faith that carried me through deep waters.

I was finally pulled into the hospital. I remember one day when my father did come into my room, somehow he did get through the front desk. I was lying on my bed, limp. He grabbed onto my foot and he said: "You are my daughter. I do want to see you get better!" I know he was telling the truth. But he could only say this in a closet. No one knew about it. I know that he meant it. His children were the most important thing to him. I heard him, but I could not respond. I knew that deep down inside this whole thing was devastating to dad, so unexpected from me, who had done so well. This is because of the false correlation that people make between weakness and mental illness. These are illnesses just like any other illness. They do not play favorites. This had to be difficult on my dad as he had laid so much of his vicarious hopes on me to succeed in a different way. It was hard on me, too, because I really wanted to succeed. I wanted to have a successful and full life as much as he wanted me to.

Dr. S said, "You need a husband that understands the illness. You do not have immediate family support." Dr. S called the television station and told them I should return to work in just a few weeks. This must have been shocking to the TV station and they must have have been wondering if they wanted me to return at all. I must say that the station was very patient and understanding and gave me longer than necessary to get back to work.

A mixed state plus an anti-depressant for me equaled rapid cycling illness; another form of the illness I was unaware of until I arrived here. I was up one day and down the next and this was tough. This rapid cycling illness was really wearing me out: up, down, up, down. Stop, please! It feels as though you are in an hourglass going around and around. My own learning curve started now with the bipolar research specialists and I owe a lot to them, probably my life.

Dr. S jacked my lithium up to about the highest level possible and I did not respond. I was resting in my room one day when Dr. S came in to break the news. He said, "I have some bad news for you, Salvina. You are not a lithium responder, but there are many new drugs out there now. You should not be discouraged!"

I knew what it means to be a stabilized bipolar and I also knew what it meant to be an unpredictable non-stabilized bipolar. I wanted to find the nearest window and jump out, but I held onto my faith, then. I also dreaded new drug trials. I was always so sensitive to the medications and side effects. Very low doses of medications had dramatic effects on me.

Sensing that this news would make me more likely to want to jump out a window and understanding that I had little emotional support from my family, Dr. S hired a nurse for his pregnant wife and he stayed with me during the most gruesome time of coming to terms with this unwanted news.

He tried me on the most recent secondary drug to treat bipolar disorder, Tegretol, a neuroleptic drug. That drug was the latest treatment. I became toxic on very low levels. I remember walking down a hallway, crashing into some lockers, and then the next thing I remember, I was in my bed and my eyes were just opening. Dr. S was washing my forehead with a wash cloth and telling another doctor in the room, "I tell you this one has been through hell and back and she is still fighting!" I still wanted life. I love life! I loved my career, please let me recover! My television career would be indefinitely put on hold! Every job that passed me by was greater than the pain. I could not wait to get back out there.

My discharge summary from this hospitalization goes like this:

Admitted: 12/12/84   *Discharged: 2/6/85*

Mental Status Examination: Exam revealed a somewhat disheveled young white female who was cooperative. Affect was labile, alternating expressions of sadness and depressed mood, with sudden hypo-manic outbursts. Patient denied hallucinations or delusions. The patient was oriented in all spheres. Her memory was intact for short and long term. Abstraction was good. Insight was good. Her judgment was somewhat impaired. The patient admitted to suicidal ideation, but currently expressed no intent. Diagnosis on admission was bipolar disorder, mixed. Hospital Course: The patient had recently been discontinued off desipramine.

Her rapid cycling picture was felt to be the result of the treatment with desipramine. The patient was observed over the next few days on lithium alone. The lithium was gradually increased up to 18-mg, which resulted in no improvement, and then 2400 mg on a qid schedule. She tolerated this increase well, with only still mild symptoms of upper GI distress and mild tremor. The patient, though, continued to evince symptoms of both manic and depressive cycling. The patient was begun on 200 milligrams of Tegretol that was increased every 48 hours up to 800 milligrams. At a dose of 800 milligrams . . . the patient developed significant GI toxicity with severe nausea, vomiting and vertigo. The patient's Tegretol was tapered and the patient was continued on lithium alone. The patient cycled into hypomania, which seemed more protracted than in the past, at which point Haldol was begun at 2 mg and gradually increased to 4-6 milligrams. Patient's lithium level at this point was 1.58 on 2400 milligrams of lithium.

At this point the patient cycled into another depressed phase and the Haldol was discontinued. The patient was observed for several days. The depression continued and intensified and suicidal ideation developed. The patient was begun on a trial of Nardil after proper preparation with a MAO inhibitor diet. Her Nardil was increased and tolerated to 90 milligrams per day. Despite a four-week trial of Nardil, the patient continued to cycle in one to two episodes per week pattern, although the intensity of her manic and depressive poles seemed somewhat attenuated as she gained greater insight into the nature of her condition.

I do not believe that last sentence for a minute. A mood swing is a mood swing, no matter how much I understand about my condition. I know I do not have control over it. I wish I did!

In those moments when I was high, I usually would make a pass at someone from the opposite sex. The libido is out of control and I remember one such day, Dr. S was in my room and I turned to him and said: "I think you are cute!" He turned around to me and said, "and I think you are high, Salvina. You will get over it." I love to be around these high level specialists that really understand our disorder because they understand and do not run from it. They know how to give encouragement and hope for the present as well as for the future. It is never hopeless to these guys. They know how to respond to your ridiculously inappropriate moments.

. . . back to the discharge summary . . . .

> *Arrangements were made for the patient to be transferred to the Affective Illnesses Unit at the nation's most prestigious research hospital under the care of Dr. C. Unfortunately, before plans could be completed, the patient's funding for hospitalization ran out. The patient was offered and indeed encouraged to accept a transfer to a state hospital prior to transfer down to NIMH. The patient refused transfer to the local state hospital, and it was decided to discharge her in light of the fact she was not able to be committed on an involuntary petition, since she had made no serious suicidal gestures in the last thirty days.*

> *The patient was discharged on Nardil 30 mg tid. Her lithium was discontinued in the last week of her hospitalization, as it seemed to have no impact on her rapid-cycling illness. Discharge medications were Nardil 30 mg tid. Discharge follow-up was outpatient care through the Depression Research Clinic with Dr. S, pending transfer to Dr. C at the NIH.*

It is good to know that there are really serious doctors out there, who not just in it for the money. They did concur that the antidepressant caused the rapid cycling. In my case, unlike many others, the treatment would make me worse at times before it made me better. I still wholeheartedly endorse the treatment of the illness, especially with those specialists. I am hoping for a cure some day. In my opinion, Dr. S was one of the two doctors who saved my life. The other is Dr. G, to whom I referred as my pretty medicine man. I called Dr. S my temporary flagpole. I always say if I had the choice between being stuck in a desert without my medications and without my doctor, I would want my medications (and water, though).

Dr. S even agreed to call me the morning that I had to take the train to NIH. Some friends met me at the station and helped me get situated at the

NIH. I could not believe that I was now at the number one research hospital. Doesn't this mean you are at the end of road and just a donation for science before checking out? There is no horizon after this. Dr. S took no money. He knew I did not have any. But once treated, He believed I had a lot to offer society. I suppose that is why he did it.

I remember walking into the living room in a conservative suit. When they asked about my mood, I answered, "I am moderately depressed today." Other patients responded, "You do not look depressed." Oddly, I never look as depressed as I really was and this even fooled some of the best in the field. "Well, I know how I feel," I retorted.

I was plenty scared, too, about my future. Maybe my parents were right. I should just hide the rest of my life in a bedroom and not seek out treatment, seek out to be better. In the so-called day room, I began meeting some of the other patients. One older and matronly patient named Eleanor shook her head and said: "Pretty Esther, pretty Salvina, what a shame, this illness." I take it she had a pretty daughter that refused treatment with the disorder. This is how I came to nickname Eleanor, mama. She told me funny stories about her daughter, typical of a bipolar in the high phase.

Manics will do some impulsive things. That is the same impulsive behaviors that someone like Ernest Hemingway displayed when he would just take off and go on a safari or to a bullfight in Spain. In the high, manics love the action and the excitement. It is the down afterwards that made him put a bullet through his brains to end his life.

This is a sad illness indeed! We lose too many talented people. Suicide can be the way that this illness becomes fatal. People cannot understand that this is a symptom of biological depression and not something you want to do. It is not a behavioral action, but a response to what you really believe. Your brain thoughts are communicating every second, "this will never change," "there is no hope," "get it over with." Perhaps by understanding the life of Ernest Hemingway, one can see and understand classic bipolar disorder.

Some of the patients in the hospital asked about my history of cycling and I responded, "Well, there were times when it was not too bad. I was three years mildly high and six months down." They all moved away from me there on the bench, knowing that almost no one they knew was lucky enough to get a three year run on a mild high.

I was still getting a lot of phone calls from the television industry. Now I always said, there is a reason they call this the communications industry. The word was definitely out that I was in the hospital with bipolar disorder! I still lived in a fishbowl. One phone call came in from my ex-husband's former mistress and a former colleague. I was definitely not in the mood for that one; assuaging some guilt she harbored inside.

I spun into a very rapid cycle; even though I was skinny, I felt like the fat lady in the circus. I was switching from the low to the high in four-hour intervals. I must have been a specimen for these research doctors, but how painful it was for me!

Then who calls, but Andre who asks, "I didn't know you were sick, Salvina. Can you meet me at the country club for a drink?"

Is he serious? I thought, what do people think? Did I sign into the end-of-the-road hospital to play golf and tennis all day? How inappropriate these reactions are. Would you ask someone else with a serious physical illness to meet you at the local country club for a drink? When are people going to get it? Send us flowers and cards but a drink. I was just as ill as someone with cancer.

"No. Andre I'm not feeling up to it," I answered.

I suppose this answered a lot of questions about the seemingly inappropriate seemingly behavioral things that happened when he referred me to an excellent TV station for a job. Glowing with a tan, slim and attractive and at this point provocative, I am sure that I did not favorably impress the station manager. The station sales manager probably heard nothing of any substance come out of my mouth. Andre knew me differently so I am sure that he had heard something that stunned him. This guy probably thought I was just another pretty face with no brains. Actually, truthfully, it felt like I had no brains at the time. I am sure that he had no plans of hiring me and still I did another inappropriate thing and sent him hot air balloons saying, "It's tough to make a move from up in the air."

I am sure he did not know what to think, but he did know that he did not want to hire me. I'm not waving, folks . . . . I'm drowning, especially at that time. Some close friends from the industry and from college appropriately sent flowers and others just did not know what to do. I tell you, please treat it like an illness, like any other because it is an illness! It is real physical pain.

I finally asked Elizabeth to take all industry calls, handle them and please not bother me with them. I appreciated that and it was the best thing I could have done. Elizabeth was a very good friend. She had a local high pressure job herself. I suppose I would not step into her current job any time soon or any job for that matter and she was making really good money now in television advertising sales.

She was wonderful in handling my calls, too. Elizabeth was an outstanding salesperson at a local network affiliate. She has finesse with people. I guess that is what made her such a good salesperson. She is teaching, now, exactly what I aspired to do.

One day she came into my room and Dr. C happened to come in. "Well, Elizabeth, after Salvina is stabilized, she will be able to have a steady relationship and marriage to a man," he said. She answered "Enough men have fallen in love with her already! She has left a trail behind her!" "This will be better," answered Dr. C. He has since become an expert in the treating drug Depakote, which would eventually stabilize me. I refer to it as my miracle drug. "She will have a normal life without these ups and downs, and a better marriage," he said.

Elizabeth lived near the hospital, so she visited frequently. Several of my friends remained loyal and visited with regularity. There was Michelle, Jean, Gloria, the English professor and Elizabeth. I hope I did not leave anyone out because those friends were very special to me.

It's a bargain I am making with the research hospital; paying with my body and blood for new discoveries that may help (or harm) me, an investment for the future generation of bipolars. It is a good deal. First, one is taken off all medications and put through a series of research protocols. Examples of these protocols would be a thirty-hour blood draw hooked up to an IV unit and spinal taps to obtain brain fluid. I had to sign a consent form to waive all liability; I was scared, but I am strong with the desire to live a quality life. I also felt that if it was my last hooray, maybe I could do something useful for others in the next generation.

After I was taken off all medications, it took a little while, but I cycled down into severe depression. I was put on suicide watch or round the clock eye contact. I was again in constant pain from my legs, with cramps, to my stomach with nausea all the way to my head.

One night I was put on a twenty-four hour blood draw to research effects of circadian rhythm. I was feeling a little high, not too high, and Dr. C was conducting the study. Dr. C always spoke softly and thoroughly explained the procedures. I was attached to an IV and blood would be drawn every half hour for twenty-four hours.

Since I was a little high, just at the point of joking, I started talking to Dr. C. I was talking about the ultra-conservative family that I came from. Dr. C, asked, "How conservative?" and I responded, "My father thinks I'm a communist because I vote Democrat." I continued to be playful that evening. I could tell that he felt sorry for me. The illness is a tragedy for all of us. He treated me like a normal person. He knew I was normal.

At the same time, Eleanor, who had been depressed the whole time I was there, had received ECT, (Electric Shock Treatments), which induced her into mania. Before she used to simply sit in the day room, saying next to nothing. Now she started moving about wildly, had her hair colored orange, was going out shopping at Bloomingdale's. She came into my room one night and told me about her highs in the past. One time she had an affair with a neighbor and could not understand why her husband was upset with her until she cycled down. She also was high when her husband died and she was all bubbly and talkative and could not control it. She was sad about that and the disease really. I didn't think that was funny, but some of her stories were.

"You know you can end up committing suicide from this horrible illness," she said, "but first, you must go the distance." She meant you have to try every drug. "Only when you've done them all will you have the right to say 'enough'."

Eleanor became a close friend and temporary surrogate mother for me. She longed for a daughter who would submit to treatment. I longed for a mother who understood that I needed treatment. We were compatible. Even in my worst depression, I would muster up a little laugh when she shared stories of her highs. The sad thing is that this is not a funny illness at all. It interrupts lives, it affects relationships and it can kill. It affects some of the brightest and most talented in the world.

I was now very biologically depressed and on eye contact for suicide. We were all going up to the gym and Eleanor, in her high state now, slapped me across the face and told me to snap out of it. I wish I could. In the down phase, I am very light sensitive among all the other things. The rays of light that would enter the room were so piercing that I had to wear sunglasses all day long. I wore thick Jackie-O sunglasses all day long and well into the evening for the duration of the mood swing. This could be why I still favor wide rimmed sunglasses. I remember the relief of those eyeglasses in those days.

Dr. C and Dr. S had different styles. I always felt Dr. C was a little tough with such a sick person. We definitely had tête-à-tête from time to time. In the end, I thought he did a good job. He has become a well-respected doctor in the field of bipolar research. He grew on me, too. One day my friend Elizabeth came in to visit me. I had heard on the TV that there was a little bit of a shakeup at her television station. She replied, "Well, you are a slug, but you are a lucid slug." By this time I could barely walk or talk and I had stopped eating completely. I am glad I could still be called "lucid" if nothing else seemed left of me. Night after night alone, in darkness, night after painful night. I did look up for my strength. We had a research meeting at the hospital once a week. Each of us got to report to the group how we were doing. It was getting to the point that I was so sick without the medications that I would just say: "Agua!" (Spanish for water) and I was asking for medications, please, all the time!

My desperation did not change the game plan for the NIH. They never let me stay in my room and sleep which was my natural inclination from this state. One day when I rebelled, I refused to get out of bed, and the staff picked up my bed and dragged me out to the day room in my bed. I was mortified. You will get out of bed at NIH from a depressed state, no matter what. There is nothing easy about these hospitals when you are used to achieving and doing well at school and work. Arts and crafts and the gym just do not cut it. I would always say: "If I only had a brain!"

I guess there were never more than seven or eight of us on the unit at the same time. The unit was run by Dr. P, probably the most famous bipolar doctor in the world at that time. He is a very personable man, as I recall. He would come to visit us each personally once a week to find out for himself how we were doing. I thought that that was thoughtful for a man so high up in the research world. He was in direct contact with each one of us. He rarely missed a week, unless, of course, he was out of the country.

When Holly arrived, about my age and also a preppy sort of girl, it was at least some companionship for the duration. We became good friends. There were several children in her family, and about three or four of them suffered from the disease. WOW! She came from a nice family. I visited them every year after I was released and better. Holly's family is a model of the genetic component of the disorder.

I remember them wheeling in another patient. I think she was the only one there in worse shape than me. She had been in graduate school when she became very ill with bipolar disorder. Her depression was so bad that they were feeding her by tubes. She was demanding euthanasia. Of course, they would not do it; euthanasia should be reserved for the terminally ill, if at all. The expectation was that once the depression passes, she would be perfectly normal. She really suffered and her condition did not change while I was there. Frankly, I do not know what became of her. I hope she recovered and went on to become a crackerjack high level professional. We were watching her waste away, so much so that they sometimes kept her outside the day room.

Back to me. I had found out I to have an MRI. By as early as the mid-eighties, they were finding differences in brain scans of episodic bipolars and differences in cortisol levels, a hormonal fluid excreted from the hypothalamus; a gland in the brain. I met all the criteria for the bipolar. I guess I could not escape this reality, so well documented. I didn't sign up for this!

I was scanned and poked until I could scream, and still no treatment. Once, when I was at my wit's end, they decided to allow a girl with panic anxiety to stay on the unit for the weekend and guess who she would room with, yours truly. I was upset and made my feelings known. I remember being outside Dr. C's office and throwing a ping-pong stick. I was upset because there was no relief for me ever from this research and I was in pain. She gets a vacation in my room for the weekend. Dr. C said, "Into seclusion for you for forty-eight hours." I responded, "That is just fine with me, forty-eight hours the whole weekend by myself . . . just like I wanted."

He must have felt somehow like he ultimately lost that one, anyway. I had my privacy, as wanted, for the next forty-eight hours. Maybe he was not so tough after all.

I sat there, in seclusion, with a nurse watching me the whole time because I was still on eye contact. Why should they lose such a good specimen? I was healthy in every respect but this. They kept me on eye contact even when I bathed; did they think I would try to drown myself?

Let's see who else was there: a budding psychologist, a foot doctor, a talented housewife, a dentist with three children, two or three multi-millionaires, a nurse, a lawyer and me-a television executive, all with everything one would want, but we had one thing in common for sure, bipolar illness. We all displayed the same symptoms when episodic.

In fact, while I was in the middle of one research protocol my doctor reminded me, "Well if it makes you feel any better, Salvina, you are in very good company." I retorted, "Yes, I know, but it does not make me feel any better." The company he was referring to was the likes of Abraham Lincoln, Winston Churchill, Ernest Hemingway, Vincent Van Gogh, Vivian Leigh, Handel, the preacher Charles Spurgeon, Goethe, Robert Lowell and many more of this caliber.

One patient kept complaining about the food. I could care less about it. Finally, one night I turned around and said, "What did you think, you signed into a country club, here?" After all, aren't hospitals known for their fine cuisine? I did not get a response. We were in anything but a country club environment. I was scared about my present and my future, night after night in darkness and overwhelming pain.

Finally my research was over and it was time for my drug trials. We were on blinds which means that we do not know what drugs we are being put on. It was a little frightening.

I remember one day, the English professor from my university stopped by for lunch. He said that he could not tell the difference between the patients and the doctors. The lab rats scored one that day! I knew from past experience each drug I was on. The side effects gave them away.

Meanwhile, Eleanor had been released virtually non-stabilized and I guess she cycled down again. In my heart, I knew she was serious about going the distance and then signing out. I knew she would leave and do it. I worried for her. I had become close to her.

I was walking into the day room for the research meeting one day and Dr. C was watching me. He really is a good guy, I thought, but I was wondering what was going on. Then Dr. C announced, "We have some bad news. Bipolar affective disorder has become fatal to Eleanor." I threw up my arms in the air and screamed, "Mama!" I was still on eye contact for suicide watch myself, but I started to run out of the room, crying, "Mama, Mama, Mama, no, no, no!"

Dr. C motioned to the nursing staff. "I have her." He followed me to my room and I asked him, "How did she do it?" He answered, "She hung herself in the basement." I answered, "Oh, no. They'll never understand that she loved life! She loved life as much as I do. They'll never understand. If I get better, I am going to make them understand that she did not want to die!"

"You are right, Salvina, they do not understand. It is good that you want to try to do something about it," said Dr. C. We were talking about the general public, our families, our co-workers and our friends. In this generation our specialists do understand; that is better than in the past. But the public still needs to be educated. It was at this point I grasped the depth and humanity of Dr. C. He was there when he had to be there.

The loss of Eleanor was a big one for me, but I would always remember what she told me about "going the distance" on drug trials. That advice actually saved my life.

I was finally feeling better, but I did not know what drugs I was on. I was getting ready for discharge and called into Dr. C's office. I was a little nervous, but I did finally feel well. I was there for nearly one year. I was afraid to leave this cocoon of bipolar specialists and patients. We had so much in common. There was a tremendous sense of relief to be out of pain, at least for the time being.

Dr. C said: "Salvina, we have determined that your illness is 100% biological. Every mood change coincided with a change in a medication. You are a keeper. Some people think that all people with these illnesses are weak, but you are strong with a highly developed sense of self-esteem. We do believe that your success has not come entirely from your illness, but that you are also a type A personality."

He made me feel so good and then he dropped the other shoe by the breaking of the blinds for medication: "You are stabilized on a combination of lithium, Tegretol and Nardil."

"But Dr. C, don't you know that with an anti-depressant in my combination of drugs I will be a walking time bomb?"

Is it possible that I, too, had gone the distance? Would I wind up a statistic like Eleanor? My time was more than up at NIH. They tried, they had done their best.

CHAPTER 6

Going the Distance

I was at the home of my friend, the English professor. I was living in the basement and trying to be as discreet as possible. My night with Andre had already been scheduled before I knew what medications I was on. I could not back off now. I was having fun at the home of my friends, but I was concerned about my future and I have always hated to be an imposition on anyone. I was always fairly independent; the thought of having to depend on others was difficult for me to face.

We would have fun at meals and no one acted as though I was any bother. All my friends wanted to encourage me to rehabilitate my life.

The big night finally came and I was to meet with Andre to talk about job opportunities. In retrospect, I think that Andre had no intention of helping me with jobs. He was really curious to see and know that I was well. Well, I was dressed to kill that night and in good taste. My hair was blown dry and silky. I wore a navy blue pinstriped suit and maroon high-necked silk blouse with maroon nail polish on nicely manicured nails. Best of all, my brain was working nicely and appropriately again. The English professor encouraged me by saying that I was a knock out and sure to get a job . . . so go get him!

We met at a local restaurant. The ambiance was nice and as usual the chemistry was still wonderful between us. I think Andre was delighted to see me looking so well after all this. I suppose people must wonder about what really goes on inside these hospitals and, like myself, wonder if the person comes out with a blank stare, forevermore. I think Andre was pleasantly surprised that night that he saw me.

When he dropped me off at my temporary home, we stopped for a moment on the steps. There had been no promise of a job or even help. I was standing on the porch and preparing to make my way inside when Andre pulled me towards him and pulled my face to look into his eyes. I was staring into his eyes and he was staring into my eyes. It seemed as though we were just about to kiss when I thought to myself, "Why ruin it now after all these years? We never had an affair!" I turned my nose into his neck and then his nose touched my neck. I knew for sure that night that Andre was one of those men that had fallen in love with me; one of those men that Elizabeth referred to, speaking of the TV industry at NIH.

That was the last time I ever saw Andre. I guess we were also saying goodbye to each other. Maybe he knew it, but I did not know it for sure. He should have just declined to see me, but I guess that he had to see me well for himself with his own eyes and not just hearsay. We said we loved each other and goodbye in the same moment, not verbally. I earned my way up the ladder the old fashioned way with hard work, talent and I was pretty-probably the necessary combination for the television industry.

My friend, the English professor, was a little surprised that I came back empty-handed. He really encouraged me before I left for this meeting. Andre was my past-tense ace in the hole, but this one-bipolar illness-was too big even for him. He could not handle it.

After six weeks, I was off to another friend's home; this time to the home of my good friend and former golf partner, Gloria. Her husband played golf with my ex. They raised two good boys. I really liked Gloria because she was practical and yet accepting. Gloria was a true friend. She always stays in touch and even traced me to Israel. I never knew how she did it. She would make a good spy. Everyone at the club affectionately referred to us as "walk and don't walk."

One day we decided to have one of the pros over with his wife. I made homemade raviolis in the middle of the night. I was starting to cycle up. The raviolis were very good, but I had left a big mess of the kitchen. We really enjoyed the night! My ex-husband's old boss always referred to me as "curly." I suppose due to my curly hair. He was another man with French heritage, like Andre and John. These Frenchman are a trip and always in my path! If I still believed in those Eastern things, I would have to attribute it to karma. We all had a nice night and people joked with me and carried on. We were completely unaware how soon the time bomb would explode. One day I was fine and the next day I found myself flying off into antidepressant-induced mania. I did not recognize it when it happened. I was so high that I had become psychotic. Gloria was afraid, but supportive. No one suspected that the episode was induced by a treating drug.

Gloria did not understand either, but she made sure that I went to the hospital. She and her husband did not desert me or take the last of my possessions contained in that car that I drove down south. These were people of integrity. They love me. They took me to the local hospital and I was admitted to the psychiatric ward. I was making no sense whatever and talking up a storm.

Gloria called my parents and asked them to come pick me up. They were on vacation and would not interrupt their vacation to get me. I had to sit tight in that hospital.

I was too out of it to even be able to speak for myself, even to say that I had been on an antidepressant and that I am very sensitive to antidepressant inducement. I was blown away into a world of my own with no support system that was able to understand my needs. I barely knew my name. I recall sitting around a circle with patients and doctors, doing some sort of psychology thing. Those things never worked for me, anyway.

It took ages for my parents to arrive, and when they did arrive, I was released into their care and on my way. This was the point at which friends were reluctant to help, it was too weird. I agree that was the most weird part of my illness, but it was also drug induced. I was a type II bipolar, which means that without the antidepressant component in my medication I only suffered mild to medium highs. But now the walking time bomb was exploding.

With their refusal to learn about the disease and their reluctance to help me through it, my parents were hardly the right caretakers for me in a crisis. Dad drove me to Manhattan and mom cooked for me, though I would hardly eat anything.

My retroactive disability benefits arrived and mom took me out to buy some clothes. As usual I purchased beautiful clothes, including a dress appropriate for a second wedding. This trousseau buying theme would be repeated in future manic episodes. Other times they were not suitable.

I bought this wedding dress in a high. I did not even have a boyfriend at the time.
It is not suitable for a second marriage gown; either.

I read Kay Jamison's memoir, "An Unquiet Mind". She had a lot of familial support. I laughed when I read her book. When in the manic stage, she often would buy snakebite kits. I guess to each manic his or her own spending habit.

I did not respond to lithium in my twenties. I've been engaged in a battle for a lifetime, but that side needs to be known, too, so people like me will not be discouraged; for the public to understand external causes of a mood swing; and for people to know that not all manics are violent.

A checkbook balance is something that can be unknown to a person in a manic episode. Spend, spend, spend, but who is going to pay for the bounced checks? I should not have been out shopping at those times. The checkbook should have been hidden from me. I think in my mom's heart, she was doing what she always thought was best for me; she just didn't understand how a manic can think.

After about six weeks, I started cycling down and I knew that I had to find a good doctor, soon. So I phoned the NIH, explained what happened and asked for a referral. They referred me to Dr. G, a doctor I would come to respect a great deal. He is one of those special doctors that cares about his patients wherever they are. I had cycled back into the down, and dad drove me into New York. I had regular appointments with the doctor because I was so down. He knew how I had been treated in the past and he thought perhaps to try a series of antidepressant drugs to see if there was one that would not induce mania. I had become afraid of those drugs. They were worse than my illness when they induced me.

My television career seemed to be on hold for even longer. I saw one great job after another go by me. It was very difficult at the peak of one's career. I saw so many opportunities go by me, like dust in the wind, one after another. When would it be my turn? I lay in my room, day after day, no one forced me into the day room, in fact, no one even came in to talk to me or comfort me. When you are out of the maddening crowd for a while, they forget about you, too.

Mom would leave meals by my side and when I did not eat, she would take them away. It seemed like a thousand years went on like this. There were those intermittent times when Dr. G was so concerned that I might commit suicide, that he would intentionally induce me into mania with an antidepressant drug. It was the bipolar form of life support. Mom thought he was crazy, but he was right to do so. I would jump out of bed and start shopping and screaming, buying five or six of the same hat in the same store. At least, I did not buy a full trousseau every time, and I was alive. "What is wrong with this doctor?" mom would think.

After one of those inducements she was so angry that she took me to a local psychiatrist who confirmed what she wanted to hear: "There is nothing wrong with her." I wonder how much she paid her to get her to say that. Once I cycled to my senses, I called Dr. G to explain my absence. Mania is difficult on the people around the patient and depression is difficult on the patient. At the next session, Dr. G called dad in and said, "Your daughter definitely has bipolar disorder. There is no doubt about it. She has been diagnosed by three or four of the best specialists in the world. Why are you and your wife fighting the diagnosis? We are doing the best we can to make her better." Dad said that it was difficult to accept, but they would try harder. He was pragmatic and he, at least, tried to listen to the doctors that he knew were good doctors.

In one of my sessions with Dr. G, he told me about a new anti-depressant named Buproprion or Wellbutrin. It was not on the market because it could cause convulsions. I knew I could not hold on much longer; my depression was not lifting and it was too serious.

The history of my illness with the mild highs and low lows made it difficult for the mood stabilizers to treat my depression, and all the anti-depressants would induce me into serious and psychotic highs. I became obsessed with finding a way to get a drug trial on this medication.

By this time, Dr. G and I had a wonderful patient-doctor relationship. I trusted him and he teased me and said that I was an honorary psycho-pharmacologist. The relationship between the doctor and the patient is really important. He is a one-in-a-million doctor. He is special. I was now determined, even from this debilitated state, to get an FDA clearance to do a drug trial on Buproprion.

You may wonder how I can say that I couldn't live much longer without the drug, and at the same time I think about suicide. When biologically depressed, one cannot think of almost anything but suicide. This is what hopelessness is.

I asked Dr. G to write a telegram to the Congress. I wrote to Congress and then I heard from the FDA. I was given clearance to try the drug. I thought that maybe now I might have a chance to be well. This was a tremendous victory; what a change from feeling as though I had lost all control of my life. This shows how strong my will and desire to live was.

We received the drug. I started taking it with some apprehension. It had no side effects and no response. What a disappointment after all that work and hope and we were back to square one with all of this. I understand that Wellbutrin does help a lot of people; it's on the market now. It is used for depression and to help people stop smoking.

By this time my disability health insurance had kicked in and they took me into the hospital to do a drug trial, as a precaution. There I met Larry, a professional and a yuppie who had just tried to commit suicide after a reactionary depression. He felt his career was over. He had a lovely wife. I became close to both of them. At times, Larry and I joked about volunteering for the Lebanon border and that would end our distress! He was blessed to have such a supportive wife and she was determined to stick by him, thick or thin. She was also a professional, herself. I admired her for that.

Larry obviously was not lazy; he had just become ill. She tried to understand everything the doctors had to say to her. They had a really nice apartment and I would go to visit them often later. I did not know how close I would actually come to living on the Lebanon border some day. I survived it.

When the Buproprion failed for me, the doctor in the hospital, Dr. G, decided he wanted to try me on Tegretol alone again. I tried to warn him of how easily I become toxic, but he did not have ears to hear, one more time, toxic.

How many times does the same thing have to happen before they stopped trying? High level doctors are always stunned to see how easily I become toxic on that medication.

In the hospital I met Andrea. She also had bipolar disorder. She had nearly died from a suicide attempt after being taken off of lithium. They had to take her off lithium because in rare cases lithium impacts kidney function. This is why doctors check your kidneys and your lithium level all the time. I suppose that Andrea felt her life would be hopeless without it. She barely survived, and then was stabilized on another medication. Andrea was a nice girl. Our dads really got on well because they were both manufacturers of clothes. They had a lot to talk about, what with it being so hard to get legal affordable help these days. I do not think either man was in favor of the unions. Neither of them had too much patience for our illness and both were clearly embarrassed by it. At least, that was the impression I received.

Between Andrea and Larry, I had plenty of good company but I just still felt terrible and wondered if it would ever change. My siblings certainly were not knocking themselves out to come and see me either. I guess no one liked these hospitals; well guess what, neither did I. Then, the time came that my insurance ran out and I would have to leave the hospital. Andrea's sister was scheduled to get married and she was more concerned that her husband-to-be would not find out about this genetic illness before the wedding. I think this is one card that has to be on the table before there is any wedding. I hear even Andrea is married now.

Dr. G said, "Salvina, there is still one more drug we can try you on. It has been used to treat epilepsy, but it is very new in the treatment of bipolar disorder; not even approved for it officially yet." "Really," I said. "What is the name?" "It is called valproic acid. Are you willing to try it?" asked Dr. G. "Let me think about it. Would it be possible to get privileges to take a short walk?" I asked. Dr. G agreed.

I was disgusted, tired and hopeless. I walked straight to the highest and closest bridge with every intention of jumping off the bridge. I stood there on that humid and hot August day just looking down into the, cool, dank water moving from the great height. It seemed so inviting, so welcoming, to end all this aggravation and pain.

But, then, it was almost as though I could hear Eleanor talking to me, "always remember, you can end up with suicide from this terrible illness, but you have to go the distance."

I walked back to the hospital and agreed to try the valproic acid. No doctor had the heart to send me to a state hospital so when they asked me if I were suicidal, they sort of half-prompted me to say "no." I said "no." It was bad enough I didn't fancy the "country club" hospitals, let alone state hospitals. I plain and simply do not like being in hospitals or even going to hospitals.

I had to go back home for this drug trial and I was in the hands of Dr. G. I purchased enough stuff to kill an elephant prepared for what I would do if this drug did not work. Twelve days later, on 750 milligrams of Depakene (valproic acid), I was well for the first time in three years. I had also gone the distance and it was a good thing I met Eleanor at the NIH. I never thought this would do it. I was one of the first bipolar patients to respond to Depakote. It is now commonly used to treat bipolar illness.

CHAPTER 7

I Could Have Been a Contender

At last better and then what! You may think that after putting all that effort into wellness, you would have earned the right to a good job right where you had left off. Unfortunately, it does not work that way. Let's see, it was September 1987 when I stabilized, I was thirty-five years old. I realized that there was, and there still is, more of a stigma in the workplace and in society than I had ever guessed. In my heart, I always viewed myself as a normal person with a physical illness, like diabetes. I tried all the rehabilitation social services agencies in the area and found that they were really more there so that they could pay their own rent than they're to help me get back on my feet.

After sitting in office after office for hours, with next to nothing accomplished, I realized this, too, was not my path to fair rehabilitation. Once again, I would have to bite the bullet because no one was going to help me to help myself. Like anything else I have ever accomplished in this life, I had to do it myself. I started by contacting a man who is a consultant in the industry and worked part-time for about one year. This helped me realize that I did not forget about the details of the job and it gave me the confidence I needed to push ahead. I was underpaid for my credentials.

During this time my beloved grandmother, for whom I am named, and who had a stroke and could not even talk, passed away. It was painful just to go and visit her before her death. I guess she had yet another heart attack and my aunt wisely indicated to the doctor, "no heroics." She passed away. Even though she was old, I was saddened by her death. I remember just standing there, holding the rose to throw into her grave and not wanting to leave her there alone. No one made me leave. They let me stand there. I think, in some way, my family did understand how much she meant to me. She was the best grandmother a grandchild could have. She never complained, even at the end.

After her death, I did receive a little money and it enabled me to go back and finish my Master's degree. I made a trip to Washington in order to speak with the department about readmission after some time. They were all so nice, perhaps a little concerned about my being able to pass comprehensives after all this time, but supportive. They were always supportive about me as a student, and I believe that they were impressed about my determination to go on despite my disability. An exception was made on length of time to complete the degree based on the fact that I was ill, with the intent of completing the degree in one year.

My parents did pay a few of my debts, but the lion's share of this illness has been absorbed by me. No help with medical bills and no help with a restart ever. I never really fully understood this. I guess there was some innate feeling that once you have something like this, you cannot really function and you are no longer worth the investment. I was just one of those that would never give up a good fight to keep my position. I was fully capable of doing my job now. The course work, as usual, was intense, at this prestigious school, but I enjoyed every minute of it. Statistics was the area most problematic for me in this demography degree. The statistics professor spent hours with me in order to see me through it.

I rented a funky and spacious townhouse with a few other students so I was right in the middle of all the action. I had a key to the study center, so I could go in there to study anytime. Several of the older students, like myself, would get together and study. It was a pleasant year and I did indeed pass my comprehensive exams. All the professors waited with bated breath to see if I would pass my comprehensives. I still needed to finish my thesis in order to get my degree, but I was already looking for work. It was great to be living in the middle of an upscale and quaint environment again. I could not believe how much the university had expanded on-campus housing.

From a stabilized state, I was performing well, even better than before. I met a few new friends and we would brainstorm together over our challenging exercises. It was an expensive, but great way to restart my life!

One afternoon, my friend Katherine arrived unannounced at the front door. She had been having an affair with a man and, once she broke it off, he tried to kill her. She was almost certain he was still on her trail. I felt terrible. I knew that if I agreed to give Katherine refuge, I was putting myself at risk, too. I decided that for Katherine, it was worth the risk. She stayed a week or two and no one came to the house. I put her way back in the brownstone and I was at the top of the stairwell. She doesn't have loose lips. She returned home and was able to get police protection. Both of us are alive and well today, but it was a close call for both of us. Maybe I read too much about laying down your life for a friend. Katherine was and is a close friend.

My friend, Michelle, saw an ad in the newspaper for an audience research specialist with public broadcasting. I applied and got the job. I remember them saying they were impressed with my Chinese language background. Well, I guess this would be my next professional adventure. They had a large television and radio research budget along with other sorts of research that I did not get involved with. Well-known people sat on our board, that much I knew. They attended several of the lobby wine and cheese parties given for supporters and organization parties. I have always been intrigued by some of them. I guess because of my parents' attitude, I did not expect to work again. I certainly did not go in telling them that I had the disorder. Even the high level specialists would counsel not to divulge the illness upon employment. People do not understand the illness. You are not hired before you even apply. They know bipolars can function at very high levels, but there is gross discrimination against people with these disorders in the world. You just need to learn to work around our disability as any other. We do have some needs. For example, it would not be good for us to do shift work. We would need to be assigned to one shift only in order to keep the biological clock intact.

Though I wrote many proposals and contracts, the organization had two researchers, one in television and two in radio, that were expected to get the money and the contracts. I had very little to say about that. They were considered to be the public broadcasting specialists in television and radio. It was a good transition job, but I was not yet back at the level of management and involvement that I was at in that hot climate market. Please remember that I am a research purist and I see no reason to pay good money for something that says nothing.

The process of rehabilitation is slow and arduous and you have to really want it to do it because the system, though getting better, still is not set up to encourage full rehabilitation. If you get sick again after three years back at work, you have to apply all over again. Once you go off disability, if you get sick again, you should automatically qualify for all your benefits, including Medicare. For Medicare, you have to wait two years. It makes no sense; if you are sick, you need the benefits when you are sick, not after you are better. There are a lot of changes that need to be made in the system and strides are being made in this area. The system must reinvestigate how to better serve the disabled so that we are not afraid to become functional again. What if we need Medicare again? Are we out on the street for two years?

One day after I returned home from work, I received a telephone call that my two-year-old niece was in the hospital with leukemia. I rushed to New Jersey as we did not yet know the prognosis. There are, I understand, two types of childhood leukemia; one is deadly and untreatable and the other, which she turned out to have, is very serious, but treatable. For whatever lack of compassion and understanding my family had towards me, they were able to understand the severity and seriousness of this situation. My sister and her daughter were given utmost attention and family members were sending her money. I could remember day after day, at the National Institutes of Health, without a dime in my pocket because my family was convinced that what I struggled from was not real. Imagine existing almost a year penniless. At least I had a roof over my head and three meals a day at the NIH; so do criminals in jail. Truthfully, my medical condition was equally serious, yet went unrecognized by my family.

I also had compassion for my niece. I was terribly upset and spent my whole two-week vacation that year with her at the hospital. It was sad to see so many children suffer. I guess it is easy to get people to feel compassion for children. Several of my niece's little friends did not make it. All of those parents suffered so. My niece did go through the two years of chemotherapy and came through with a clean slate. Of course, she will always have to be checked. I thought if my niece did not make it, my father might just die. He was taking it so hard. My paternal uncle is a research oncologist and he was right on the case from miles away. I suppose had he not gotten on the case, it is possible she would not have done so well. My mother was devastated that her granddaughter needed chemo, understandably. I followed with a short two-week mild dip into depression.

I returned to work with my vacation taken and still hoping the best for my niece. I was working really hard at my job while trying to complete my Master's thesis. The department chair was demanding, a tough cookie, and we had some disagreement about the emphasis of the content. Another professor, who obviously understood her better, mediated between us. It turned out that I nearly had to complete two papers in order to meet the requirement. I did get an "A" on that final thesis. All is well that ends well! I graduated in spring 1990. My parents came and were very proud of this accomplishment.

Slowly, slowly and agonizingly I was climbing my way back to full functioning again. It was a lonely battle because there was no one there to help and support me. On the job, I was meeting other researchers and once again forming good relationships in my field. I would entertain in the townhouse. It was spacious and sparsely furnished. I can remember having over 20 people there at a time for a party.

Public television and radio chose the nicest places for conferences. While I was working with them, we went to the French Quarter of New Orleans and Monterey, California. I flew into San Francisco to see my aunt and uncle in San Rafael and then I rented a car to drive down the coast to the conference. It was a gorgeous ride and Monterey was equally breathtaking. I also visited Tucson, Arizona, for the first time while working with them. I remember flying in, renting a car and arriving at the hotel. At the desk of the hotel was a card describing what a scorpion looks like. Being a city girl at heart, I proceeded to check my whole hotel room, including the bed for these creatures. These trips helped to keep me interested in a job that was not quite stimulating enough for me yet . . . .

It was good to see that I was taking small time-zone changes well, too. You see, I was taking it step by step and little by little, almost with fear and trepidation at times. All these were baby steps towards "total recovery". With each success, I would say to myself, "Yes you really are better. Yes you really beat this thing!" But, I was about to have the ultimate test.

I really do not know why, but a sudden loss of medications upset my system and caused some short-term psychosis. This was a setback. I was back in the work environment getting restabilized on my medications and knowing that any sudden interruption in my activity would be bad for my stabilized state. When things got real bad, my good friend Jean took me to the hospital. I was so scared that she offered to stay with me. I think she must have realized how it must feel to have that door slammed and locked behind you; no exit.

There are rules for surviving on these wards, too, and it is best to learn them quickly. Jean flew me up to New York to get me in touch with Dr. G. My parents met us at the airport. Dad was really impressed by her friendship as she would not take any money for the paid flight. We waited forever in the emergency room and then went home. He shared with her his concern for my future security. Most of my bipolar friends had special financial provisions made for them by their parents.

I worked hard and long hours and I was plenty competent for what I was hired to do. I really liked all the contractors I worked with. At any rate, it was a starter job, if anything. I was under employed compared to previous positions and hoping to move up later.

I started looking for work and was successful; after a few years, I was promoted into a new job with a major producer of children's television. This would require another move. I guess this is why I never had roots, moving from one town to another all the time. It was an exciting job in an exciting city. I made $20,000 more per annum than at my last job.

I moved up and found a roommate that worked in the production side of television. We shared a spacious big old apartment on the Upper West Side. There is something very charming and alive about working in production. I owned a lot of black dresses and coats and somehow this was very appropriate attire for the area.

I felt immediately at home again with energy surging through my veins, always hoping that it would not turn into too much energy.

I became very settled into my apartment and living in this wonderful location. It took me all of about two weeks to figure out what happened to several programs due to our target audiences. The other parts of departmental organization were going fairly well here.

There were implications across the whole national television system for the problem with our programming. The networks had already conducted quite a bit of research through something called the CONTAM study to examine the related issues. I was careful to examine our data, read the CONTAM and then called the researcher that commissioned the CONTAM study and asked for a meeting with him in the office of my boss. My boss was reluctant to act. At any rate, we had the meeting with Bill, one of the better known researchers from a major network. He pulled me aside after the meeting and asked me if I was happy at this company. Clearly, he was very impressed and would have tried to get me into a network position. I was, at the time, very happy so I foolishly declined. I really wished I had a crystal ball. I was not looking for attention. I was looking for results and action. That is the way I am put together; if it is broken, let's fix it now!

I was invited to the next public CONTAM meeting and I was making more and more contacts. I knew that I was allied with a man I had only ever heard about as the guru of television media research. Would I have the nerve to go in and talk to him about this matter? Yes, he is the best in the television-marketing field, the leading media researcher; I set up a meeting with him. From the outside, his reputation was so inspiring that I could barely see shy-me going to see him. I went in with a presentation prepared and some other comments. As I was in the elevator, on my way up to the executive floor of the big black rock, my heart sunk to my stomach, my knees were knocking. I do not get anxiety attacks, but I could barely breathe in the elevator. I thought to myself, I might not be able to talk when I arrived in his office. After all, this was the one media researcher who could make you or break you in my field. He's the best! The meeting went well. I came to have tremendous respect for him. Meeting him was the highlight of my career in television.

The truth about me is that I am usually trying to help someone other than myself and that is probably a fault because most other people are always trying to help themselves. Perhaps over the time I was there, I developed some feelings for him, the first man in my age range. He is really smart. He really knows how to deal with people, too. He really knows the business. We did a lot of parallel research without knowing it. Meeting and knowing someone like him was far more interesting to me than most people because we understood the same industry in depth. I saw someone who was the best with the least loose lips in the business. I saw why he was the best.

Another network started a committee for children's programming and I was asked to sit on the committee with the top people in the field. It seemed that I was finally coming into my own as a television media researcher. Several years behind me now and I was really looking forward to my future.

I was kept traveling a lot, too. I was always on business in Santa Fe, Aspen, Phoenix . . . but we were up working by 5 a.m., even on those trips. Some of my family was jealous, but I worked hard and rarely got to see much of the area I was in. I was giving a lot of presentations. This is a business where the show must go on. I was definitely commanding respect in the business.

I think by now, except for taking my medications, and getting my blood work for my level and liver tests, I almost began to forget all that pain and that I ever struggled so hard just to get through the day. I was making it in the number one market and you know what they say, if you can make it there, you'll make it anywhere.

My boss and other executives knew that I did understand ratings. I loved this arena. I finally saw that you could be scholarly and also part of the television ratings business, especially if you concentrate on methodological issues. I have a direct style of communication. Some people cannot take it, but it is one of the normal communication styles. I tried to make as best an adaptation as possible for personality differences and communication style. I understood the differences, but it is more difficult to make unnatural adaptations.

It seems like I was just getting my feet wet when everything went up in smoke. It was May 1992, close to five years since I successfully stabilized and I had remained well. I went on a business trip to Toronto and I did not have my sleeping pill, Restoril, with me. I started cycling up somewhat. I lost a lot of sleep at that conference and that is bad. At the special dinner concluding the conference, I was sitting with all the most powerful men in the industry, except my favorite that night. His right hand man took me out after the dinner and I remember telling him all about the reorganization in detail. I do get talkative when I am cycling up. My libido was escalating, too. I am glad I did not do something I would not have wanted to do. He is maybe the most gorgeous man in all of TV media research. I am glad I exhibited control. I hear that he has left his position and is working with a ratings company now.

All these intelligent and good-looking men were fun to be around. I finally found the right mix between academia and application for me in a job and it all fell apart overnight. Despite the fact that most people in my industry would say that I am very talented in my area, my long-term career dreams would always elude me for one reason or another, especially because of my illness.

There is something special about meeting the number one man in your area without blushing, though I do not think he ever saw or even knew that. He really knows what he is doing. He was the male focus of my last mood swing, my last trousseau, in the spring of 2002. He was only in my mind, then. It is a good thing I did not call him during that swing. Who knows what I might have suggested?

I was trying to reach Dr. G, from Toronto, but I was in another country, how could he get this controlled substance to me? I had a slight hypomanic episode. It was not severe, but I did write some inappropriate correspondence to my boss and say something I should not have, which is a symptom of the high phase.

Some people are normally this rude. But my illness was used against me. My doctor had written a letter to explain the circumstances. Then the company wanted a second opinion. I went along with the organizations second opinion request. I had to get all my old records, even from the National Institutes of Health. I knew I was fine and that bipolars can function at a very high level, so technically there was nothing from my point of view to hide. The organization was playing hardball with me, though. I was also in contact with the NIH at this time.—A social worker from the NIH was encouraging me in the background. She has always been so encouraging to all of us. I think that everyone in the medical field was sorry to see this happen after such a long stretch of a good record.

It only took me a few days to be back to a level state. Really, a mountain was being made of a mole hill. I passed my second opinion with flying colors. However, I did not stay. One day, the second opinion doctor, called my office and said, "Yes you are fine, but you should consider a fresh start."

We still have no power, no voice and perhaps even what we say is held suspect with diminished credibility due to our diagnosis, but our specialists know that that should not be the case. I was perfectly capable of performing my job. After I left, I was not re-employed in New York. I suspect my career was ruined by that incident. I should have taken Bill up two years earlier.

I could have been a contender for sure!

I feel I had been treated unfairly. I still feel that I made it in my own right.

I grieved the loss of that arena. It was the perfect mix for me: practical and academic.

CHAPTER 8

Ten Good Years in Remission

I guess there is a realist in me. I recognized that there was no point in fighting and when I am well, I am very capable of taking care of myself. I was doing very well from September 1987 until December 1997 as far as bipolar illness was concerned. I was already planning to go for a year of Jewish Studies. I was off to Chicago. I would live for one year in a women's residence on the Gold Coast of Chicago. There were a lot of young women here and older women in transition, and it was in a lovely part of Chicago. I was learning more and more about Jewish history, too, and developing a greater and greater interest in going to Israel to do some genealogical research at the Diaspora Museum.

I was learning about Zionism and the history of Israel as well. My interest was becoming stronger and stronger to go to Israel. Would it be possible to trace back my roots? I had no idea what kinds of documents my family had.

I have relatives there on my mother's side and I had some other things planned for such as a tour. I planned a short-term trip for the summer. The political climate for the summer of 1995 was very tense. Israelis were split on Prime Minister Yitzhak Rabin's plan to exchange land for peace. The most religious Jews were upset about this and protesting throughout Jerusalem with signs and shouts. Sadly, this ended, as you know, with the shooting to death of the Prime Minister in November of 1995. I remember seeing his granddaughter saying in Hebrew, "Sliha, Sabba. Forgive us, Grandpa, that we did not take these life threats seriously. Forgive us, God that we did not foresee this." She was asking for forgiveness from God for not being more perceptive about the reality of these threats the previous summer.

I was still level. I was putting on weight, something that could have caused another disorder. I suppose this was an emotional reaction to my dad's death. I did feel alone now, except for God.

About this time, the National Institutes of Health contacted me. They wanted to use my case as a case study as a successful patient for the use of Depakote. I gave them permission to print my life chart in a research report. I was considered to be a real success story! So stable, so functional at the time.

I left for Israel and began my visit in Haifa. I then traveled south to Tel Aviv. I could not believe how easily I fit into the country.

I visited my mother's family near Ceasarea, Israel that summer. It was good to see that I had family there. Since they live close to Caesarea, we had dinner along the shore.

I moved with the same pulse as Israel. I loved it! I was born to live there.

I went home and began asking for all family documents so that I could return to do the research. I began research on my family and also on what the television industry was up to in Israel. Perhaps this would be the fresh start that second opinion doctor was talking about? It certainly felt like home for me. I found one document where my mother's family originated in Spain and it traced generation by generation and a name change. It turned out to be even closer still.

I went back home and started working in a guesthouse on Manhattan's Upper West Side. As usual, it felt wonderful to be on the Upper West Side again. Every day, there was a routine to checking people in and out of the guest house and then we ate as a family in the kitchen downstairs. This was fun and sort of like I had a new family. Mrs. Walden, the woman in charge, was so sweet and so motherly. I found it heartwarming to work for her. Her husband suffered from arthritis, but she managed to help him and also deal with everything related to the house. I guess I was there for about three months before I was scheduled to leave for Israel again. The brownstone was decorated in a lovely Victorian motif and old enough not to have an elevator up five flights of stairs.

I had periodic meetings with an Israeli woman in the broadcast industry in New York. She understood the market in Israel and knew that the People Meter was about to go into Israel. This was a system that I knew a lot about and it is still considered the world standard, despite numerous measurement problems. No doubt with all my experience, someone could use me in Israel. Even the best in the US have mentors and know they need good training in everything.

I was planning my takeoff for early January 1996. If you remember, we were snowed in big time in the Northeast and I believe I may have been delayed by a week to two weeks on the takeoff. I do not believe that I ever saw so much snow. I was back at my mother's home in northern Jersey for the takeoff from Newark Airport. Actually, I had packed with me a lot of family history, for this trip to Israel, including this interesting document which documented my mother's family Spanish heritage. Some of her documented roots go all the way back to the time of the Spanish Inquisition, on both sides.

I was trying to get myself to Tel Aviv where the majority of television and advertising takes place in Israel. I was concerned about time zone change. Three or four hours is okay, but as bipolars we should take as much responsibility as possible for our wellness and the management of our illness. Our doctors should help us coordinate these things. These factors are very important and not yet understood by the public the way the public understands that a diabetic cannot have chocolate on a regular basis. Please take us seriously when we say something is not good for our health. At the same time, we should take every possible precaution to stay well. It takes more than just the medicine, but also discipline in other areas of our lives as well. I know the general public has a long way to go on understanding how to intervene.

I started looking for a temporary place in Tel Aviv. The long term apartments come without appliances or anything and most landlords ask for one year's rent in advance. I was on Ben Yehuda Street for two to three months, in a nicely furnished business apartment and I began making my contacts in the television industry. The applications come right out and ask you how old you are! Cultural differences are often amusing at first. I remember going to the supermarket for sugar and coming home with salt. One day, I was driving before I learned to read Hebrew and I was driving the wrong direction on a one-way street. The policeman was getting so frustrated trying to get through to me that he just let me go. I was beginning to understand the struggles of new immigrants to the United States more. My landlord told me that I could do better and to keep an eye out for a better deal.

I decided to start studying Hebrew at an intensive-language Ulpan in Tel Aviv and I was meeting people, new olim, new arrivals that way. I arrived just in time for the series of terrorist attacks following the death of Rabin. It was nearing Purim, the holiday celebrated from the Book of Esther. It is one holiday where the children dress up and everybody is expected to have fun, to commemorate all the times in which Jews were persecuted and, nonetheless, the Jewish nation has survived.

Due to a former American and then Israeli physician, Baruch Goldstein, having gone into a holy place in Hebron on Purim and massacring praying Muslims, Purim would never be the same in Israel. Yes, there is extremism on both sides of this issue. For a while, Hamas and Islamic Jihad, both terrorist organizations, seemed to especially like to ruin Purim. In March 1996, I was only a five-minute walk from the terrorist attack in Dizengoff Center. I saw body parts of women and children flying in every which direction. I do not mean to be graphic, but that is what happens during these suicide bombings. I was on my way home from visiting the Association for Americans and Canadians in Israel, an organization that assists immigrants assimilate into Israel. I remember walking down Allenby and then turning right to make my way down to Ben Yehuda Street and my apartment. The next thing I remember, the bomb went off. I heard the explosion first, then tried to see where it was coming from.

I lived next door to a group of fairly young Mexicans who witnessed the bombings and several were in shock. I had witnessed the death of my father, so I guess I was somewhat hardened. I must admit I called home screaming and my mother did say that this was the first time I ever seemed upset in Israel. I was keeping a good eye on these young people, though, in case I thought they required medical attention. Their parents called and were very upset. I think they wanted them to come home. The repercussions for these acts are more widespread than can be imagined by the news.

At any rate, I was very touched by this experience and I wrote about it in my journal the next day:

March 11, 1996—Tel Aviv, Israel

Now I know why they call it terrorism. It is because they want to paralyze a society with fear.

It was the most awful thing I have ever put my eyes on, save the death of my dad.

Maybe I was being prepared. Now I am just beginning to understand that the mention of peace brings more violence. When will it end over here?

Today I have a whole new perspective on the land for peace process, one I will chew on for some time and never take lightly. The young Mexican Jews eventually went back to Mexico. Israel isn't for everyone.

I called my uncle at work to relay what I saw and he replied, "It happens every day here." People get hardened . . ."

I guess that I would, too.

Since 9/11, I suppose, Americans have a better idea of what it is about. I was deeply disturbed by that and the way I handled it was by going into seclusion and writing a poem:

November 16, 2001

The City
that never sleeps has a nightmare.
do not stop short on the street
or you will be carried away
by all the people you meet,
people of every shape and size . . . .
the city
south is anywhere
south of the Lincoln Tunnel
anyway
who heads south
when Sylvia's north is uptown in Harlem
never lonely
always moving
the doorman is your best friend
Your hairdresser your only confidant
the City
that never sleeps had a nightmare
on the morning of September 11, 2001
screeching voices
a moment of despair burning bodies
falling
falling
falling into an eternity
that only God knows for sure.
The city that never sleeps
went into a coma that day.

I continued my interviewing for work, searching for my roots and studying Hebrew at an Ulpan. Except for taking care of myself, bipolar illness was a thing of the past for me. It was now 1996, almost ten years since I had had a major mood swing.

Someone I knew was vacating an apartment in Herzliya. Herzliya was named after Theodore Herzl, the father of Zionism. It is a nice suburb of Tel Aviv and the apartment was spacious and rent was reasonably priced. My small-furnished place in Tel Aviv rented for $1200 per month, and in Herzliya I would pay only $650 per month, paid in advance. I had to believe that I would be staying in Israel at least a year. I moved out there and it was really nice. I bought new appliances, but used furniture. I even had my own dishwasher now. For the first time in my life, I had a really nice, comfortable apartment that felt like home.

I was in a family neighborhood with good people all around me. It was not a dangerous area, though any Jewish neighborhood could be a target for the terrorist groups. It is a young country that culturally, in many ways, reminded me of America in the fifties.

My neighbors were lovely people, like most Israelis. Those born there are nicknamed Sabra, after the local cactus, prickly pear, indicating that they are "thorny on the outside but sweet on the inside." Personally, I think they are more sweet than tough.

Finally I had a meeting with executives of a major network station. At that time, that was the only commercial station in the country, still affiliated with IBA, the Israeli Broadcast Authority. The president was definitely interested in my working for them, but he had to wait for his research director to return from maternity leave. As a foreign resident, I needed a work permit. In the meantime, another company was starting a new product and offered to procure the work permit and hire me for a lower than the going pay; this is normal practice in Israel for first-time jobs. I later reconnected with the television station, when the research director returned from maternity leave. I liked her and she seemed to want to treat me fairly.

I felt like I finally found my home. At least, I felt like I had many friends in Israel. It is expensive to live in Israel compared even to exclusive parts of the United States and the average income is low, so many Israeli Jews are needy as well and few people realize this. I worked for television, but delayed payment until I could get the money legally.

I was adding furniture to my apartment, still without air conditioning in this hot country. I had a lot of visitors in that first year. One young girl that was making aliyah (Hebrew for Jewish immigration to Israel) was going to room with me but she had trouble sticking to the rules for my much needed sleep. My Israeli doctor—a very good doctor—finally wrote her a letter, but he said, "If she does not believe you, why should she believe me?" He could not understand why I would think it would have more credibility coming from him. I responded, "Maybe she just thinks I am crazy. That is what she is telling the whole neighborhood."

I had to ask her to leave my home. It was unfortunate, but that is what finally happened. She is now a citizen and doing well, I presume. I wish her all the best. She was young. As we mature in life, we understand more and more, but we are unwilling to receive that wisdom in youth. What is that phrase, too bad that youth is wasted on the young? My dad always suggested something like that.

While she was still living with me, another girl who had worked as a journalist in the United States arrived to make aliyah, Sarah. Sarah and I share some good immigration stories together and we are about the same age. Sarah and I had dinner at a Tel Aviv Chinese restaurant. It was amazing. Sarah told me that night that an executive at the Israeli Advertisers Association thought that my heritage stemmed from the time of the Spanish Inquisition. He was knowledgeable in this area. I shared with her that I also believed so, and that I was in the process of establishing the facts. We became friends, and she helped and encouraged me to write this book.

Moving to a new country is difficult. I remember one night when she invited me over for dinner; we went out to grocery shop and she wanted to buy a chicken without the neck. She kept motioning to the man behind the counter moving her hand across her neck. I just stood there smiling relating to each attempt.

I hooked up with a genealogist in the Galilee. She was meticulous about record keeping. It was amazing the things that they had uncovered already about Jews left in the care of non-Jews during World War II. People involved in these kinds of persecutions would try to find clever ways of leaving clues for posterity about their Jewish roots. I was enjoying my research with this woman and at the Diaspora Museum. The Diaspora Museum in Tel Aviv has a wealth of information about Jewish roots and names. This museum is located near Tel Aviv University.

I was also working hard at my jobs. I had bought an old blue Fiat, for which I probably spent more on repairs than on the purchase. I should have probably bought a new car. It was always breaking down with one thing or another.

Rosh HaShanah, the Jewish New Year, was approaching. My next door neighbor always made the most delicious homemade honey cakes, traditional food for the holidays. She used to say, "There is no such thing as a Jewish princess in Israel." She is right! I had to tiptoe past her door because she always cooked tempting and high calorie food and she was very hospitable. The Israeli people are incredibly hospitable. There is a sense of unity because of all the trouble in the land.

Israeli women definitely work hard. You can eat off of their floors, not only during Pesach (Passover), the holiday for which the house must be super-clean. The women my age were still baking and making homemade Shabbat dinners every Friday night for their families.

I spent Rosh HaShanah with my family and Yom Kippur by myself in prayer and fasting at my home. On Yom Kippur, you can hear a pin drop in Israel. It was the most serene thing I have ever experienced. Lurking behind the scenes on that holiday was the awareness of potential enemy attack. Israeli soldiers needed at this time are exempt by Jewish law from observing the holiday.

My doctor was amazed and remarked at how stable I was on my medications. I followed all the other rules about time zone change and uninterrupted sleep as well. In fact, I was rigid about it. I never wanted to be sick again, never, never again, please! I think those high level specialists that really understand the illness underestimate how little the general public knows about it. I was beginning to feel very, very comfortable in my apartment, perhaps the first time that I really felt like something was mine. I was, in some ways, growing attached to it. I am not particularly materialistic, so this was unusual for me.

In November, my mother traveled to Israel and I met her at Ben Gurion Airport. As a mother, she sensed that I had finally found my niche. She could tell that I was truly happy. Despite our differences, I think she would be able to sense this about me. She did not like the shuk, the open market, and wanted to get away immediately. I tried to tell her that she was having a cultural experience. She did not want to hear it; she thought the food was filled with germs. She and a friend came to stay with me after their tour. We did a lot of things that were not included in their tour. Even she indicated that Israel was, in many ways, the best-kept secret. I think she liked it.

During my well times, it was not that difficult to get along with my mom. I am able to care for myself; in fact, I am actually independent. We had a good time together on this trip. My mother wants her freedom; she did not want to be depended on. She craves for her own life now. She was always meeting the physical needs of a large family and she feels that finally now is her time.

My mom was leaving and feeling satisfied that I was indeed happy living in Israel, happier than she had ever seen me. I was a natural fit.

I did not have any problems with klita (integration). Yet, my battle to live there was another struggle. I had to prove that I was Jewish and that was not easy to do. I did not take the creative short cuts to citizenship that were placed before me. As everything else, I did it the old fashioned way, honestly. Sometimes the rules of admission into Israel seem arbitrary to me. Many Russian Jews have long lost their Jewish identity, yet they are entering the country in enormous numbers. I was considered as born Jewish everywhere in Israel, except the Ministry of Interior.

I experienced two mild earthquakes while I lived in the Tel Aviv area; one was centered in Cyprus and I do not remember where the other came from. Both times, I remember being fully aware that the earth below me was moving. I went to Ulpan (Hebrew class) after one such earthquake, and we were discussing earthquakes in Hebrew that night. The word for earthquake is reyidat adamah (literally, "earth tremor.") The other time, I was in a tall building at work in Ramat Gan and one could feel the whole building swaying.

For Passover that year, I had about five invitations to choose from. Israelis will never leave you alone for a holiday. Even my boss invited me to his home. His invitation was the most enticing, but I went with my family again. My family also had an annual Thanksgiving party with a lot of friends; mostly American-born Israelis.

I was beginning to work more and more hours for the television station without a work permit. I had not yet received a paycheck, and I had to come up with a way for them to pay me legally. I somehow was led to believe that if I started an overseas consulting firm, this would be enough. I really taught them a lot. However, I later came to realize that when an American professional joins a local team, he or she is considered a threat.

Meanwhile, my friend Sarah met a nice sabra man in Israel and they were married. She was studying Hebrew and getting freelance writing jobs. She was doing pretty well for an olah; it takes a while to get established and even longer usually for mature women. Their wedding party in Jerusalem was an experience. A friend loaned them a beautiful mansion; there was classical music and tastefully done food and a wonderful atmosphere in the middle of this suffering country. I think every faction of Israel was represented that night, including people from the Palestinian Authority. Sarah and Yakov are very special people. I started to share my life experiences with Sarah and she encouraged me that this was a story that had to be told.

In the summer of 1997, I decided to make a trip back to the United States to establish an overseas consulting firm. I decided to stop in London for the time zone change problem. I was booked on British Airways and would return in early September. What a sad time to visit London for the first time, just when Princess Diana died, and people from all over the world were there to pay their respect. I saw more of London on the return visit. I took an open-air tour bus and saw some of the most important sights. I also took a boat ride down the Thames, a wonderful experience. Of all the cities I have visited so far, London is second only to New York for me.

In the US, I visited family and friends in New York City. Mom took everyone out to dinner. Maybe she felt somehow relieved of me with me living in Israel. Soon I was anxious to get back home, to Israel. Now, in September 1997, I could say with confidence that I was ten years in remission. Unbelievable. I barely even remembered or thought about my past episodes in my daily living anymore. I just took my daily medication and had periodic blood work done.

CHAPTER 9

The Nearly Fatal Twist

I think by now I had developed an undiagnosed case of sleep apnea. The additional weight I put on was certainly a factor. With sleep apnea, a person stops breathing in the middle of the night for a short time, blocking the oxygen from reaching the brain. Often this causes a brief awakening. When combined with bipolar illness, sleep disruption can induce mania. Gradually my bipolar disorder was being destabilized. I was slowly ascending into a high; the signs were there. I was buying beautiful, but unnecessary new furniture. I was more irritable and my energy level was escalating. This is only the beginning before you spin completely out of control. My close friends and acquaintances knew that I had bipolar illness, but no one recognized the early symptoms.

This is a real problem because people do not recognize it until an advanced stage, and then they do not want to talk to you anymore. We really need the public to recognize the symptoms and learn how to intervene as you would any illness, early. The most obvious sign that I was cycling up was that I installed a shower stall in that apartment, which I did not own. As my friend Michelle remarked, "You do not even take showers, you take baths. Why would you install a shower stall in an apartment that you do not own?" Only someone experiencing the high would use this type of bad judgment.

I was unaware of my worsening condition. In hindsight, I am surprised that someone close to me could not tell. Maybe they could tell, but did not know what to do. This would begin a six-year cycle of high highs and mild lows interspersed with about a two-year normal state.

Remember, at first you are in control and even more "on" and then you can spin out of control. I spun out of control and then it became obvious. I went into a state of paranoid delusions. Unfortunately, left untreated, this thing becomes worse. I just know that people would never leave someone who just went into a diabetic coma on the ground and step over them, but they still do not understand what to do with us. I was still even unaware that it was the sleep disruption that precipitated the mood swing. Some friends tried to help, but no one knew exactly how.

As my mood swing became worse, I was scared. My body functions were no longer normal. I could not eat and feel right. I started to experience paranoia, thinking that someone wanted to hurt me. My sister in California sat on the phone for twenty-four hours one day, just talking to me. She could tell that I needed help, but she did not know what to do. Another friend finally realizing something was seriously wrong tried calling my doctor. No luck. The doctor was headed out of town for a conference. I believe he told my friends to take me to the emergency room. My roommate was doing her best to understand what was happening to me, but in vain. She also tried to call my doctor. I was not an Israeli citizen yet, so maybe the medical community did not want to admit me for financial reasons.

This was a critical point, an out of control point, at which someone had to effectively intervene. In my life until recently people have not come to my aid in time.

My friend Rachel finally brought me to the emergency room of a hospital in Tel Aviv and they just released me as though it was nothing. The next night, I was so afraid that someone was coming to hurt me that I took an overdose of Tylenol and Depakote. After that I was finally taken to the emergency room at one of the best hospitals in Israel. I was in critical condition for a few days, and they were not sure whether my liver would make it. Of course, if my liver did not make it, neither would I. This was not a suicide attempt. It was an action taken out of the fear of paranoia. In my mind, I was trying to beat an imaginary killer to the painful punch. My condition should never have gotten this far.

My sister had finally talked my mother and my brother into going to Israel, but they arrived too late. I was already in critical condition. The emergency room should have caught on. My friend and nurse knew it was a psychiatric issue of manic-depression. My mother gave my Aunt Rivkah money to buy me food and special things and to keep an eye on me. Then she and my brother returned to the United States. They left the country while I was still in critical condition.

The hospital put me on eye contact, but I was not suicidal. They still do not understand that because of the lack of initial treatment, I cycled into an extreme psychotic state. This is something that could have been avoided. I almost died due to lack of knowledge about what to do and the lack of understanding of the seriousness of my state. But we who have this illness have no power or voice. I spent another four weeks in the hospital getting restabilized on my medications, which were no longer in my system. My friends were nice, coming to visit me, but I was still not well.

At the hospital I met new people. One girl had bipolar disorder and her family was very supportive. She was high and obnoxious but her family said that she is really a nice girl. I believed them, I knew how obnoxious one can be when in the high. I am not offended by high people. I understand them. I knew that she was probably a very nice girl. I always envied the small number of bipolars that did have supportive families. It makes it difficult to have compassion for us, though our specialists do! Her father said it must be easier to have an illness like this in the United States, where people are more accepting. Let me tell you, in my experience, it is never easy to have an illness like this.

By the time I returned to my apartment, my roommate had moved out. I guess all this was very traumatic for her and just before her wedding, too. Truthfully, it has been determined that this mood swing was caused by sleep disruption.

After I was released, workers in the supermarket referred to me as *meshugene*, Yiddish for crazy, right to my face. I was a regular and good customer! I can imagine what was being said behind my back. Bipolar illness is no different than diabetes or high blood pressure! This is why education on this illness is so important. How would you like to be called crazy to your face in a store where you regularly buy food?

I say there is much to be desired in the knowledge and understanding in the United States; but even more so overseas. My doctor was the chief of unit that I was on and he returned from his overseas conference. They waited until my liver enzymes were normal and then decided to put me back on Depakote. After I was stabilized, I was still not feeling like myself, but a consensus was reached that since my liver had taken so bad a hit, it would take me some time to feel better.

I was released and I found it difficult to care for myself. I contacted a volunteer organization to try to get someone in to help me get meals, etc. I was still on a special low fat diet. I did get to go to my roommate's wedding and I thoroughly enjoyed it, although I felt as though I was being set apart. No one was talking about me and the family was doing the best to treat me normally, though I am sure that no one understood what really happened.

It is amazing that I lived long enough to eventually figure it out with the help of expert doctors. It sometimes feels as though you are a detective to think back and track what happened.

I found a woman from England through some volunteer agency. She had had some digestion problems in the past as well. She was a live in, and everything seemed fine at first. Then, Saddam Hussein started getting his feathers ruffled again. I already had my gas mask ready. This woman had the news on, it seemed like twenty-four hours a day, all different stations, on the radio and television. I just wanted sheket, quiet. I was very weak and she made me go out and buy the materials to seal a room. I did not mind getting her a gas mask. The Israelis around her were going about life as usual but this woman was freaking out. Not everyone can live in Israel; you do have to be able to live with constant threat of one kind or the other around you.

One day, not even thinking of it, I shared how all this happened. Well, the fact that I had manic-depression, you would think I was a freak! She began belittling me around my friends. I thought, what is wrong with this woman? Well, twenty-four hours before the Hussein ultimatum, we got her gas mask and then, the next morning, she took off for England and told me she'll send me the money for the gas mask. She never did. I finally decided that it would be next to impossible to get foreigners to stay in Israel at such a tenuous time.

It is even more tenuous now. The fact is, it is always tenuous for one reason or another. Frankly, if a scud missile was about to come flying through my window, I did not even want to know about it. Ignorance is sometimes bliss.

Sometimes, I think the movie King of Hearts was right. The ones who are diagnosed with these illnesses are the sanest of all, and the rest of the world creating wars are truly crazy. Pedophiles roam the streets, churches and other socially acceptable places, but we are to be feared? I have never once done a violent thing to anyone, not even an animal.

In early March 1998, two years after arriving in Israel and after much work to make a life there, I would be returning to the United States for an indefinite period of time. This one was a heartbreaker to me. I loved living in Israel, despite the dangers. I reluctantly and sadly made my reservation to go back to the United States. Once again, my life would be put on hold for this illness. I was still not really cognizant of the cause of the break. I would only put the pieces back together later.

My mother seemed more open than usual to have me come home and to try to help me. My brother picked me up at the airport. I had already e-mailed Dr. G about my medical concern for having become psychotic overseas. We still had a good relationship and he did see me almost as soon as I returned to the United States.

Psychosis was not typically part of my illness. Dr. G wrote a disability letter for me and I was put back on disability and rightfully so. What was so difficult is that after ten years of good health, I would have to wait another two years for Medicare medical insurance. No protection of the hospital for me. Also, at this time, Medicare still does not pay for medications and these medications are expensive; they can cost half your disability check alone. Something has to be done about our medications. I know that some proposals have already been made., but they weren't enough.

I felt like I was back at ground zero. After all, I had gone the distance and for this to happen? My internist was still concerned about my being on Depakote so we were starting new drug trials. It was awful. I was having all the bad side effects again and some drugs that are supposed to be better, make you feel like a zombie.

I had slowly come off the Depakote and my system had a tough reaction to it. Without medical insurance, I had to do most of it on my own, from home. I was monitoring my own blood pressure and trying to do everything that the hospital would do. My mother was taking care of the diet and the cooking and she was really trying. I know that Dr. G was doing me a special favor by understanding that I had no health insurance.

I was at the beach house, in a moderate level of depression and I was actively suicidal. I spent a lot of time with a friend of my mother's, Adi. We went to thrift shops together and bike riding; she was a lot of fun and a little zany! My mother was good to me that year, 1998. My mother and I had a nice year together.

I remember one day when Adi went up a one-way street the wrong way and we were approaching a jeep with teenagers. The faces on those teenagers should be in a movie or on camera. Adi just shrugged it off as a mistake anyone could make. She is different, rides a junk of a bicycle about eighteen miles a day. Maybe it was easier for my mom because Adi spent so much time with me. Adi found the best clothes at thrift shops for next to nothing and dresses that way. She really knows how to negotiate and live on a shoestring and she is not poor. My mom and I ate with her a lot that summer. I had no car and by 6 p.m. would just go into the back room and listen to the radio. I was seeing a few friends once or twice a week. I was doing the best I could. I was bored and scared, too. Would this be another long haul? I did not know. It was, sort of.

By the winter, we were back in northern Jersey and I had nothing to do and no car. Friends of mine in Israel were able to sublet my apartment furnished so at least I did not have that worry. I just let them sublet the price of the apartment, and threw in the furnishings hoping that they would take good care of it. I knew they were responsible people. That was one worry off my back for the duration.

I thought I had already gone the distance, but these new drugs were not better than Depakote. I had a three-month supply of Restoril, ninety tablets at 15 milligrams. I just kept looking at it. I had, after all, gone the distance once. I thought, new drugs? I wonder what Eleanor would say?

Due to the fact that my ammonia levels were high, an internist and digestive specialist wanted me off my miracle drug. Against my better judgment, I tapered off slowly and my body was having a difficulty in adjusting after all these years. I fell into more severe depression, as expected.

I was at my mom's house in northern Jersey. The people responsible for my suicide watch went out to shop for lawn furniture. Eye contact means just that, a person needs someone to watch them around the clock.

A trained person would have had me on eye contact around that clock. I was talking about it less and less because I was getting more and more serious. I had believed that this was all behind me for good. I had believed that I had beat it. No one seems to understand how important it is, when someone needs to be watched for possible suicide. Andrea Yates is an example of someone who needed eye contact from post-partum depression. Perhaps five children are dead due to lack of public awareness. Normally, we turn on ourselves, but she must have been frustrated. One cannot even take care of oneself, let alone five children. Where was the system on that one?

I know nothing about the case in Texas, but I do know this, she should not have been left alone with those children in her condition.

Now those children are dead and she is in prison for life. Perhaps she became frustrated caring for the children when she felt so sick and perhaps there were people around her that minimized her pain and inability to properly care for them. There usually are people like that around. We usually turn on ourselves and not others.

When someone is in this state, it is a serious matter. The biggest symptom that kills a bipolar is suicide, a symptom, not of behavioral, but of biological depression.

While my eye contact team was shopping, I seized the opportunity to check out from this world, or so I thought. I was tired of this; you just cannot imagine. It is worse than anything else I have ever suffered from physically.

I swallowed all ninety pills fully expecting to open my eyes in heaven. Instead, my team returned in time to find me barely breathing and they called the ambulance. I was in intensive care and also on life support. I was in a coma for about twenty-four hours. They told my family I would likely not survive, but if I did survive, I would be on kidney dialysis the rest of my life.

I never expected to open my eyes on this earth and I was very disappointed when I did. My mother almost immediately told me that Dr. G was no longer willing to handle my case. Wow! I lived and my kidneys are fine. I repeat, my mom is getting better in understanding this illness. Dr. G always said I had an honorary degree in psycho-pharmacology.

I still felt that my mom would like to push me into a closet. She liked the idea of 6000 miles away; let it be someone else's problem, not hers. In a shoe box of an apartment, by myself, and set apart for disabled and old people; just get in the closet. Her sister agreed.

The loss of Dr. G in my life would be nearly as great as losing my dad when it came to this illness. He had always been behind the scenes as my flagpole. We shared such a special patient-doctor relationship, and now that was over, too. I hear the best doctors take things like this the hardest; perhaps he felt it was a breach of our longstanding special relationship, but it had nothing to do with him. I just wanted out, finally, no more war with this illness. I had already gone the distance, in my eyes. I was initially angry that I survived.

I really did not want to live any longer with this illness. I was transferred to the local psych unit and I do not think I ever really showed much enthusiasm for going on.

When you are in a coma, everything is black. That was my experience, anyway. My family says that they were talking to me, but I heard nothing. I understand my sister in California, upon hearing the news that I would likely not make it, fell to her knees upset and crying. She really loves me, but has a family of her own and she lives far away.

I returned to my mom's home feeling defeated that I could not even succeed at suicide right now. Ninety Restoril tablets is not an attention-getting technique. It is a checking out technique! Just like Eleanor, I thought I was checking out.

I am glad now that I made it through that time and the one after. I know that it is only by the grace of God that I am alive today, so I guess there is a reason for it. Maybe I had to tell my story. It was not my time to die. They did put me back on Depakote, a wise move to keep me alive.

My liver made it and my kidneys made it just fine. I came out of it in remarkable condition. Although I did not need dialysis, I had temporary incontinence and I had to see a urologist. My mother would start screaming whenever I had "an accident," which usually happened on the way to the ladies' room. Luckily, this was very temporary. She should have been grateful that I survived and not on dialysis. She made it clear that she did not want me with her all day. She must have hoped for a halfway house; back in the closet with me.

I started one of these partial care programs and felt very much like I did not belong there. They were really set up for behavioral problems. I felt bored and out of place there, but they had to do something.

After a while I started feeling like myself again with the desire to go on. I volunteered at the hospital. I was now feeling close to myself, as far as mood goes, but I would have probably cycled back naturally, given time. After the kind of manic episode I had in Israel, it is only normal to go down. I was still on Prozac, working in the hospital daily, studying Hebrew and doing well, in general.

I had been put on Prozac, an anti-depressant drug. Well you know from my history that this would be a temporary solution only; remember the walking time bomb story? Keep in mind that I had severe sleep apnea, too. The doctor, my new local doctor, Dr. B, prescribed it for me. He had me sign a waiver for release of history.

Soon I began to think about my life and my home in Israel. I was missing the life I had built up for myself. Was I well enough to go back? The answer is yes. I was well, but I should have been slowly tapered off the Prozac before the trip. I should have been monitored for a little while off the Prozac. My history clearly contra-indicated an antidepressant drug for long-term treatment.

I do not know why I did not think about how harmful it was for me to be on Prozac. The doctor was apparently oblivious to the danger to me. I was not taken off the Prozac and he cleared me to go back to Israel. It was only a matter of time before there would be a repeat performance on that medication. Any halfway decent doctor who saw my history of anti-depressant-induced mania would have never put me on the drug, let alone release me to go back to Israel shortly thereafter on the drug.

I started making my plans to go to Israel. My good friend Jean would come with me. We would stop in London for the time zone change and then in Greece because Jean really wanted to see it.

I was leaving behind my brand new car with the thought of shipping it with other items. I had no idea my brother would decide it was a loaner until I shipped it over.

Well, we were flying El Al into Tel Aviv. I was a little apprehensive with all that happened to me in the past. We were bumped up to the business class for lack of space. It was exciting to see the approach over the Mediterranean. I do love Israel and it felt like I was coming back home.

I seemed to handle the time zone change fine; this was mid-April 1999 now. I had been well again since about Christmas. We landed at Ben Gurion Airport and everything was fine. I rented a car and took Jean around the country on our own. I even drove down through the Judean desert. I remember one tour bus driver shocked that a woman could maneuver all this and he screamed at me: "Kol ha Kavod," literally "all the honor" but meaning "that was spectacular." I like to drive and my motor function is good when well.

We arrived back at my apartment and we cleaned it all up. She was going to mop the floor, but in Israel this is done with a pole and a big thick rag, is called sponja. She would not believe me that they had no American mop in Israel. She made me drive her around to every household goods store in Herzliya, but finally she started sponjing. I reminded Jean that she was having a cultural experience. There are a lot of cultural experiences in Israel. I only lived in the country for a few years and kept a nice home. Luckily, most everything was kept in good shape. I had a light teal glass coffee table and it was broken. I had bought it as I was cycling up before I left the country, spending being a symptom. I really liked the table and it matched everything else so nicely. Jean said the sublet tenants should have offered to pay me for the table, but it was not worth ruining a relationship over. The story of my life. People destroying property and not making retribution. They took good care of the apartment while I was away, at least.

I just let it go, again, and knew I would never recoup any of that money. Everything else was in order and well cared for and I am sure that other things were accidents.

In Israel, there is even a word for being too fair or one who would rather err on the side of being overly fair to the other person or neighbor; it is called being a frayer. No one wants to be labeled frayer in Israel. And yet there are very lovely people there. It means a sucker really. I guess I am a sucker and a bipolar. At least the term bipolar does not define me in its entirety . . . in fact, not nearly.

About mid-June, I started cycling up, due to the combination of the antidepressant drug and sleep apnea. I was definitely out in the shops buying up a storm again. I was getting up early and walking on the beach with a neighbor. I was still at a good point. I had just purchased a brand new air conditioner, a big and powerful one, for my apartment and it was great! It was worth the US $2000 alone. Finally, I did not need to sweat through the summer. I was settling in, so I thought.

On July 8th, I spun off into severe and psychotic mania. I doubt that two sleep-disrupting phone calls alone would cause such an episode; it had to be the anti-depressant this time. Why didn't I remember? Why did Dr. B let me come to Israel on this drug? Jean could tell I was sick by the phone calls I was making to her home in the United States. She was trying to help by telling me to call my doctor in the US, but it did not compute in my temporarily disabled brain because I had a doctor in Israel.

As it often happens with people in that condition, I started communicating excessively and obnoxiously with people. It started with an e-mail to a man who was a my former roommate's good friend, and this made him hostile. From a well state, I would never say anything about my former roommate causing me to become ill. Well, he worked with her, and before you know it, everything was crazy while I could barely stand up straight. Everyone backed off. No one helped me this time. In fact, ultimately some people really hurt me and caused my mood swing to accelerate.

The problem is that the mood state is so offensive and no one seems to believe that the person cannot control it. But why would anyone do this stuff on purpose?

Just back off and help the person get help.

There is loss of censorship control when you become high and you need medical treatment. I always wondered how Winston Churchill, who lived on the high side, was able to maintain his political career as a non-stabilized bipolar. Nurses at the NIH told me that he had a good team of censors around him.

A good censor would have stopped me from sending that first e-mail that caused all the other confusion and hurt on all sides. Actually, I could have used a good censor on several occasions in my life.

I would get upset if someone was very obnoxious with me for what would seem no reason.

There was a reason.

The manic person that is subjected to anger and confrontation will almost always get more high and obnoxious, maybe even violent. My neighbors were trying to help me as best as possible. It is unfortunate that I did not have someone around me who understood what my immediate medical needs were. None of my closer acquaintances was helping me. I suppose that the obnoxious symptoms of a manic were more than they could handle. Once again, it is tough to love and be concerned about someone in this state.

I was vegetating in my apartment trying to figure out what to do. What Dr. S told me fifteen years ago rang true in my ear, "You need a husband that understands this illness!"

My doctor for manic depression was out of the country. In the summer a lot of people travel. I went to another regular doctor and he sent me to a local hospital emergency room. I took a cab to the hospital fully expecting to stay. They did not catch on there and just released me.

I went back home barely able to stand up. This was a month after I cycled into severe mania on July 8th. I must have walked around the country for a whole month in this state. Even Dr. B said, "I can imagine that you would have burned a lot of bridges walking around in that condition for as long as you did."

You just need to take some time to read about symptoms and you should not treat a sick person that way. Perhaps, because this happened before their eyes, episodes one on top of another, they wanted no part of me. I can separate myself from it and realize that from their perspective, it did not look good.

The truth is there were reasonable medical explanations, through no fault of my own for these breaks, and they were serious and scary for me.

There was still no excuse for what was about to happen to me. I would lose everything I had worked so hard for again; my apartment, my home. The people involved can have no idea how much more they depersonalized me through their actions. They must really believe that those affected by bipolar illness are subhuman and somehow unable to think for themselves. In not so many words, this time my illness gave some people a license to steal with no conscience or seemingly so. They have rationalized away what was really done, believe me.

My neighbors decided that I needed to go back to the United States, if only so I could get the help I needed. They decided to have me buy a round trip plane ticket from Israel, so that no one would question my leaving. It was crazy! I was about to board a flight back to the United States and I was not even cognizant of what I was doing. I bought the non-refundable round trip ticket for about US$1500.

The day before I left was very interesting. My neighbors downstairs started taking advantage of my debilitated state, buying my belongings for far less than what they were worth. They had me sign off each item. They had to know I was not well enough to do this at the time. Later they even acknowledged that they knew I was sick, but they somehow felt certain that they did a good work, mitzvah, by getting me a little cash in my pocket for the trip. Actually, long before the middle of this pillaging event came to an end, a so-called friend came to my apartment for me to sign off my old car that I had given them. The car could not be signed off that day. She saw what my neighbors were doing and she stopped them. She said to me that they were not happy that she showed up. The ethical thing to do right there, in my opinion, would have been to get someone to help me to get my other things back and simply lock the door and wait for me and my family to decide what to do with my things once I arrived in the United States. The rent for the apartment was paid for three more months.

What were they possibly thinking?

She did convince me to pack two suitcases and not just one. She was putting some of my things to the side for a shipment, but at the same time she was pulling paintings off my wall for her daughter and filling her car full with other items. I remember telling her that I could use my microwave in the United States and she responded, "It is too late, it is already in my car."

They did take me to their home for the night, and drove me to the airport, but this must have somehow made them feel entitled to my possessions. It was a nightmare; they knew I was sick. He was well aware of what was happening, so they were gentlemen robbers, what can I say? I felt raped. For the most part, they are probably scattered throughout Israel now. I understand a big hole was left in the wall where the air conditioner had once been. They have my air conditioner and have never paid a cent for it. My family kept getting a communication that there was nothing of any value in my apartment.

This was simply not true. I have a documented inventory of what was in that place. I had an appointment for the assessor to come the week I left for the United States. What a way to treat a sick person! I have heard stories of other bipolars being taken advantage of in this same way in the US. My mother paid for the dining room table to be shipped to the US and two chairs were left there with no attempt to return my mom her chairs, actually my chairs; those chairs are still not here. But there has never been an attempt to make any fair retribution and there appears to be no remorse.

Meanwhile it took me until the end of October 1999 just to cycle back down enough to know that I was back in the United States.

Toto, we are not in Kansas anymore!

I guess, as my friend Michelle always says, we are in a time that is "all about me." People, in general, are self-centered, looking out for number one. When my friend Jean visited me, some time later, in New Jersey, she said, "That man definitely stole from you. Just remember he stole from God and there will be consequences for that." I believe there will be a day of genuine justice, so I can let this go, too. But justice will reign someday.

Unfortunately, I would now cycle in different phases of a high, mostly hypo manic or mildly high for a full year, with the tail end being the worst. Once again an antidepressant drug spun me into a rapid cycle or rapid cycling illness, the most severe form of the illness. I no longer had Dr. G and this Dr. B was not for me. Really, I needed to be with a high level specialist, a good one. I had no idea that I was still high, even in the low high, it is difficult to know.

I was, however, now cognizant of all that transpired in Israel. Another tremendous loss. This time a life built with an inheritance that I might never again get; a life that I loved. Can you imagine changing countries without knowing it? By the time I cycled down, I could have just sat down and cried for hours.

My mother did not want me to live with her again, so my friend Marilyn let me rent her apartment for the winter. It was nice of her to let me rent it at a price I could afford, way below market value. The house is located on one of the more upscale beach resort areas of New Jersey. Marilyn and another friend, Becky, insisted on taking me out every night. They did not understand the illness, but they were compassionate people.

This time around I found out that I had good friends who put other people first. It was only in retrospect that I realized that I was rapidly cycling again. I was in different phases of the high for a full year before I cycled down into a mild depression. I did find good help at another Ivy League Hospital. I will never be put on an antidepressant drug again.

Decision: No more anti-depressants for me.

Due to this illness, I would become accustomed to hurts, disappointments and financial losses. I learned what it was like to lose. I learned what it was like to be disappointed. I learned what it was like to feel lonely. Nothing in my childhood or early adult life prepared me for that.

The deep waters are the illness, but moreover a failed marriage, no children, an outstanding career ruined, loss of loved ones, all the major life changes. They are stressful, many unwanted months, years on the sidelines. Still, I have had a fascinating life and I am still alive. When there is life, there is hope. The hand was gasping to get the head above water while I waited for the cure.

CHAPTER 10

Good Friends are Hard to Find

Becky and Marilyn really watched over me for the nine months that I lived in Marilyn's home downstairs. She has a duplex on the same island where my mother has a home. I came to terms with what happened and went along with their program, getting involved in activities. I was not depressed then. I was just mildly high and writing well-written letters . . . everywhere. I was hoping to regain my credibility.

Shortly after I moved into this new home, I learned that my best friend while I was growing up, Carrie, was dying. She was happily married and doing well professionally as a college professor and potter. She was at the height of her career when she was struck with cancer. I was trying to keep communications open via e-mail. Sometimes she was receptive and sometimes she was not. I did not take offense. I knew she was suffering and in denial until the very end about the outcome. She was special in my life; another painful loss. When we were children, we were never apart, even on vacations. She was the little blond girl in between the feet of the movers when we moved into our home.

In my own life, I was struggling to stay stable. In the fall, Marilyn, Becky and I went to a class on Monday nights. These people also run a wonderful school and some upper class men were making a trip to Israel. I was asked to teach about Israel once a week. I was grateful for the invitation because it helped me feel better about all that happened. The teacher who was taking the students was a widower who had graduated from a school I respect. He was really nice, too. My Uncle Bobby visited in the summer. He can relate to and love everyone. I talked to him a lot during his visits to the beach. Just like with my dad, I never lost credibility with Uncle Bobby. He knows that I am honest, maybe too honest.

I was relatively normal at this time and there was, I believe, a mutual attraction with a man I met. I soon forgot about all that transpired in Israel. And then it happened again. I popped up into the high phase and wrote him a stupid letter. It is always someone in the high phase. It was not meant to be, I suppose.

Becky and Marilyn would check on me daily and we would go shopping together, too. I grieved yet another loss, sort of. That really hurt me. Well, after all, I need people around me with an understanding of bipolar illness. My mother eventually showed that she did have some understanding.

Becky and I went to see her daughter's plays and concerts at school. In the back of my mind, I never lost the desire to return to Israel, even now.

After "the incident," it was more and more uncomfortable to go to the school. This was the second man in just a few years that I did this to. Do people think I am aggressive or boy crazy? I am not; I was high.

As I said in the introduction, there is always some man when I am high. I bought a trousseau again and dreamed of a wedding. Making a pass at a man is a sure sign that I have become high. I would never do that from a well state. I believe the man has to make the first move, always.

When the winter was over, I had to leave Marilyn's home so she could rent out the apartment on a weekly basis. I lived in my mother's beach home for the summer, but I was in that elderly and disabled housing by the fall. It was depressing and not suitable for the previous Italian American princess. We just never know what this life will bring our way. At that time, my mother still had little patience for this illness.

By October, I cycled into a mild down that typically follows a high. We were going to have to start drug trials. Michelle did not want me to be alone in an apartment during those trials. She knew that I was very sensitive to medications. Her husband, my former boss, agreed that I could go live with them during the drug trials. I was so tired and not looking forward to more drug trials. The first few drugs did not mix well with valproic acid or Depakote. I was having terrible side effects. Finally, a small dose of lithium mixed with Depakote made me feel more normal. I thought the battle was won for a second time. Lithium is a mood stabilizer and not an anti-depressant, and so is Depakote. I breathed a sigh of relief. Dr. BA, was getting to know me.

My friends Mark and Michelle have an eleven-year-old son and I began to play with him. I tell you, depression makes you feel that you must have been bitten by a tsetse fly. I was in one room knocked out with my depression, and Mark was across the hall knocked out with the flu. We were both heading downstairs frequently for water. Dry mouth accompanies depression and the drugs do not help.

Mitchell, the eleven-year-old son, seized this opportunity to go into business for himself. I guess he reckoned that neither one of us in our current conditions really wanted to make the trip downstairs for water. He set up a water stand perpendicular to the two rooms and charged a dollar a bottle. After I recovered, I taught him the principles of wholesale and retail. Mitchell and I enjoyed one another once I was well. I started cooking family meals. I really appreciated that this family did not let me go through this alone. I felt loved by them and it felt good. It is important to feel loved. There is a great Proverb; it goes something like this, "it is better to live on a roof than in a house with a contentious woman." I am not contentious. I was still living in the cardboard shoebox at home; that was depressing enough. It was across the bridge from the beach house. My mother, I think, was happy to have her freedom. My journeys had taken me here, there and everywhere, with no roots, disjointed. Even at my worst, I tried to keep my sense of humor. Mark and Michelle are special friends even today. Jean is still a special friend, even today. They have really stuck by me through thick and thin. Becky and Marilyn remain special. Several more are in that category. The English professor also passed away a few years ago, but remains special to me.

This depression, as most depressions, was accompanied by ruminations about what I did in the high phase. I was so embarrassed about this nice man and my inappropriate advances. If nothing else, I would have liked to be friends, but I guess it was not meant to be. If people really understood this disorder the way our specialists do in this generation, we would not have such serious misunderstandings. Another loss. More pain. I care about people, even to maintain a proper friendship. This illness, when episodic, can be a relationship buster.

Well, when I was feeling better, Michelle and I threw a dinner party for mutual friends from the very beginning of my career. It was great. I helped with the cooking. I love to cook! Mitchell was shocked that anyone could cook without a cookbook. Michelle said she always uses a cookbook, so that is like magic to him. A handful of friends have made it their business to remain good friends. I felt loved with Michelle and Mark, and that is half the battle. The other big half is medication.

Just before I began school, my friend Carrie died from cancer. I was devastated by her untimely death. She was too young. She would not even let me visit her towards the end. I cried a lot. More pain. Abba . . . father . . . please. I do not know if I buy into such phrases, "no pain, no gain," or "adversity builds character," remembering what Andre once told me.

Soon after Carrie died, 9/11 happened. How tragic, and it still has repercussions. I started crying when I saw the World Trade Center go down. In reality, it hurts today. I love Manhattan and always will. My father would be shocked to know of the world situation today. Since I spent so much time there, it hit me hard. The whole thing was incomprehensible. It has changed the way we view things forever here. We Americans are not used to this kind of thing happening on our soil.

Now that I was well for six months, I started to review my options for another rehabilitation. A Master's Degree always seemed to be the path to satisfying work. Perhaps another degree? Finally I made the decision to go to back school. I felt well and stabilized.

When I returned to school, I took 5 courses, probably too heavy a load. Also, a professor at school was really applying undue pressure on me and treating me unfairly. I was starting to ascend from stress for the first time. Once again, I did not realize it was happening. This would turn out to be the big one that introduces my story.

I was getting to school on time. I was in a very conservative and fundamentalist circle and some people there had peculiar ideas about bipolar illness that have nothing to do with the medical reality.

In the second semester I cycled into a very high manic episode and eventually went missing in New York. My mother was frantic while I was missing and after I got out of the hospital, she wanted me to live with her. She has changed about this. She wants to learn about my illness. She acknowledges that it was real. She has been coming to Philadelphia with me and learning. She recognizes that something serious can happen and she sees that this genetic disorder is seeping into others in the family. She is reading about it now. I have been doing that all my life. I do not understand why she is so concerned, but I am happy she no longer thinks that I am faking.

Structure and reasonable hours are best. You need a support group of good friends who will not be afraid to intervene when necessary. What you don't need is intervention by friends who do not understand it to be a real medical illness.

Two families with children also sort of adopted me and we did things together. Children are wonderful. This is the one thing I sometimes wish I had had.

Back in Pennsylvania, I was making a lot of friends and, naturally, a few enemies. I was going to art exhibits and concerts with good people. I was planning a trip overseas with two friends and I was contented with shalom in my heart, most of the time.

The situation started to escalate and so did I. There was a considerable amount of sleep disruption. I guess I will always have close calls. I must stay alert, and so do family and friends. There are people that do not care if they make someone sick.

I was walking on a street with shops, and I almost went into a bridal shop. There was a check in my spirit. No. I do not need a trousseau. But what does this mean? I should have known here that something was going off balance.

Then one day, my libido went out of control and I fantasized about a younger man that I was working with on a project. I stopped at my friend Patti's home and started talking about my fantasy. It was graphic, and she said, "Salvina, this is not like you. You better take these thoughts captive and call your doctors in the morning."

I knew it was time to turn myself in to my team, Dr. BA, and Dr. J. I spoke with Dr. BA by phone and she put me on a low dose of Risperdal to nip it in the bud. When I talked to Dr. J, I said, "I surrendered early this time." And Dr. J said:, "This was not a surrender, it was a victory! Stay in close contact." Then she asked, "Did you do anything to hurt yourself or get into any trouble?" I answered, "No. I never called him about this."

A person in the high phase can get into a lot of trouble and burn both bridges and money. When a man comes on to women in an aggressive way we call that rape; but when a woman comes on to a man, that is called an affirmation and never reported. Even this is not behavioral, but symptomatic of a grossly increased libido. It should never get to the place where I make that pass. We just recently made a second catch before the libido increased. Another victory. I also am being treated for sleep apnea which should help me to control bipolar disorder. We are having more and more victories than defeats by catching it early. It doesn't have to control you. With a little help from caring people and specialists, you can control it.

People need to understand how not to make us sick and how to help us catch it in time. I have come to protect my health at all costs, and that is good. I never got sick again. I am well today in mind and spirit in 2006.

CHAPTER 11

An Ivy League Certificate of Sanity

I am really blessed to have had the very best of medical care in my life. I have heard horror stories. At least I was treated like a real person by the medical community. Even the glorified baby-sitters were trying to get me out and work with me.

Now we have organizations and associations to represent us, but, in my opinion, consumers are not there yet. There is the MHA, NAMI, DRADA and DBSA and more that are out there to help us. They help some but we still need to work hard on the rehabilitation aspects of this illness and on the stigma. We need parity in insurance and in salaries, but it is getting better.

I started to interact with some of these groups and found they were doing some interesting things. A group of us were being taped for a mock job interview where one story ended in a state institution. I heard stories of gang rape and other horrible things like sitting in feces. I know that my doctors were looking out for me in a very special way, and God's hand was on me. I think our specialists are great and, in the next generation, the general public will have a better understanding. All it takes is wanting to know about it.

Through knowledge, we can help others and ourselves. We have seminars and support groups. Things are getting better all the time. I have been better for over two years now and I am learning how to avoid the things that make me sick.

Anther woman's experience: She was set to go to the creative high school in Manhattan. Then she fell into depression and had too many shock treatments. Her dreams were lost. So many dreams can be destroyed by this illness. I am glad she could not see my face when she finished. I was crying like a baby. It is so sad about the tragedy of this illness.

She asked me for a ride to NYC afterwards. I drove her there. I was so upset about her treatment that I stopped along the way to buy her dinner at a nice restaurant. I really sounded like my dad this night and said: "Have whatever you want." We went into the restaurant and she ordered salmon for the first time in years.

She must have wondered why anyone would treat a "nobody" like a queen for a day. Maybe I even felt badly that, unlike her, I had received such outstanding care and was treated decently in hospitals.

I was so moved by her story. She shared more about what happened to her in state hospitals. I thought again about my aunt and wondered about her life inside those walls. What did she really die from? Nobody talks about it, really. I just hear that she slumped over in the dining room from a heart attack. Why did she slump over? She should have been told: "Do not let them take your dreams! Do not let the situation go that far! Strive to be the best that you can, despite your handicap! Do not let it become an excuse for laziness, either."

We who are affected with bipolar disorder still need better and truly effective rehabilitation programs. We are still on our own, and to avoid experiences like mine, we need other options than dependency on the kindness of strangers. We need our families to be well informed and supportive. My family, thank goodness, is much better now. We need less stigma to be able to work.

Three prestigious and Ivy League hospitals treated me. That should entitle me to an Ivy League Certificate of Sanity. How many people have that kind of proof of sanity? Yet, if my illness is known, who would hire me?

The medical care I received helped me always believe that I could rebound from this. It kept me always optimistic about the future. They continue to help me to be optimistic.

My family has come a long way. My mother and I have been attending DBSA support groups and now we are in the initial stages of starting a group on the Island, the Island of choice now.

I love it here now.

I no longer feel exiled.

CONCLUSION

My mother's beach house is the place I found refuge in sickness, at least when I was allowed to stay there. I came to love the house in off-season—so quiet within ear reach to the ocean all night. It helped to be exiled here. Besides, I made a lot of good friends here, too. I have always had friends. I have been well for over two years now and counting. I will always need medications and to deal with maintenance, but I think I will be well. I have no patience for people who say it is not a real illness; I would not wish this one on anyone.

A few blocks from this beach house is the best pharmacist in the world. He was most helpful during my time of disability. I think he knows how every drug interacts with another. It is a local ma and pa drug store with personalized care. I knew he was always on my side. He is a still a type of security for me.

And lastly, I need less time now with doctors and pharmacists. I still need my medications, but my drug trials are over for now. I would rather be productive myself, as always. I'm working hard to improve the lives of people living with these disorders.

At 50 things start changing for everyone. Some people really start having bad health. I have some other minor health problems, but I am taking good care of them. Now it is the uphill battle to regain my life, rehabilitation again. Call me a dreamer, I would love to work again.

My mother and I have made peace with each other and have found understanding. While my mother will never understand what is to walk in my shoes, she realizes I am a strong woman, and like a phoenix I get stronger as I continue with my recovery. We have become friends now, my mother and I, taking solace in each other's company. She has become my friend.

Total recovery takes the cooperation and acceptance of outside resources, trusting for employment. I am looking forward to the future. I sleep with the sounds of the waves brushing against the shore and knowing that I am here for a while, committed to setting up a support group. Everyone has gotten to know me here. The corner restaurant is like a second home. They catered for me a few times and also treat me like I am somebody, always. I needed that then and I need that now.

I feel prepared to help others.

This time, my return is on my own terms.

I am not a controlling person, but I like to be in control of my life.

Hopefully, that element of control is back for good. After all, I did not surrender, I was victorious this time and hopefully forever now!

The ocean is so beautiful and it did not pass over me. I'm walking in the surf looking back into the distance that I endured and traveled.

I am a survivor.

ACKNOWLEDGMENTS

Thanks to the lighthouse, which represents my spiritual journey and final revelation of truth. May everyone find light and peace there.

Many thanks to the bipolar research specialists without whom I would not have lived to tell this story. They always treated me like I was valuable, like I was somebody. They never minimized my credibility. We are the most disenfranchised of all society to many segments of society.

Also thanks to a special social worker at NIH who does a lot of work behind the scenes for many of us.

Much appreciation to my sister from California and her whole family who have given me a lifetime of support and encouragement.

The same goes to my older brother who always reassures me that he would never leave me without a roof over my head. It helps, when you have a disability.

Many thanks and love for the handful of friends earlier on and in the present that have stood by me in good times and in bad.

Much gratitude to a handful of my mother's friends who tried to entertain me while I was ill and treated me as a human being while I was sidelined at the beach. You know who you are.

A great deal of appreciation to two fine writers for encouragement and assistance, Phyllis Coe Nevins and Jan Jaben-Eilon. Jan read and re-read, edited and re-edited the manuscript She gave me advice on books to read for some Israeli portions of this book. She never stopped encouraging me to stay with the project. Phyllis Coe Nevins gave encouragement and support at the onset of this project in 1989.

Many thanks to all bipolars, without whom the world would be a more boring place. God had some purpose in making us, too. May this project help us all to become humanized, in some way.

Much appreciation to the stimulating arena of esoteric television media researchers who provided the work challenge that suits the typical bipolar.

And last but not least, to my family. I hope this sheds some light on my life and thank you for starting to show a desire to learn.

ADDENDUM

Tips on Helping a Bipolar in Distress

Some bipolars are in denial about their illness and actually resist getting help from anyone, even doctors. This is the most difficult bipolar to intervene with from the outside. Additionally, the system is set up with hippa laws that make it very difficult for someone from the outside to intervene. These laws strictly protect the confidentiality of the patient, which is good, unless the patient is too sick to realize they need help. So, for example, should I become manic, but not realize that I am manic, the system makes it very difficult for anyone other than myself to get me into a hospital. This has, in reality, happened a few times in my life. The State of New Jersey has passed a law in which mental health advance directives can be stipulated and held in your doctor's office, so that this detail can be overridden by giving limited power of attorney to another person. This seems to be working well for me, though I have not had to use it. They should pass this bill in every state.

A person in the high phase needs as little stimulation as possible. This person is already energized and needs calm. He/she should be isolated as much as possible until someone can get this person to a hospital. Even though a manic frequently thinks they do not need a hospital, he/she needs a hospital for effective treatment. The intervention must be steadfast with pointing the person into the hospital. It is not an easy task, but it is doable.

Do it with compassion and kindness. It is best not to argue with someone in the high phase as it will only exacerbate the swing. The person may become verbally aggressive. Do not argue back. If violently aggressive, you can call the police to intervene and get the person to the hospital.

A person in the down phase is fully aware of the pain that he/she is in and usually wants help at this point. The inclination, though, is to stay at home alone and sleep. One needs to ascertain if the person is suicidal or not. If the person is not suicidal, they should consult their doctor to see if a medication change is in order. Intervention can be as simple as keeping the person busy until a new med kicks in. If the person is suicidal, he/she belongs in the hospital where "eye contact" is more easily employed. This means watched twenty-four hours a day. This could be the difference between life and death for someone in this state. This state is horrible to be in and almost nothing but treatment can make it more bearable, in fact, eradicate it.

Every bipolar is different, but what has worked for me is to have a psycho-pharmacologist (medicine doctor), a cognitive therapist and a support group. Also, a person living close by who can recognize a problem before it is one . . . . is very helpful. This designated person must be willing to learn about the illness.

The components that keep a bipolar well go beyond medication alone and more and more is being learned about that. It can be very serious and life-threatening, so we need to be sober about it.

The basic components are:

proper medications and proper medical treatment
a good counselor
8 hours sleep each night
be careful about time zone changes—coordinate with doctor
good diet
exercise
a peer-led support group

Sometimes these medications slow down the metabolism so it is important to diet with exercise, too. Anything that you can do to assist a friend stick to the regimen is helpful. Peer-led support groups that are now popping up nationally through the Depression Bipolar Support Alliance is great for that. These groups have veterans at the helm and in the trenches who can share personal experiences. If you have a friend in need, point them to the website : DBSAlliance.org and go to the map to find a support group near you or your friend.

The most important things one can do to help a bipolar is to love him/her as you would anyone else and to be a facilitator in reducing the stigma of having the disorder. Acceptance by the general public would help all of us to be all that we can be during our lives. Isn't that what everyone wants?

We will probably have some down time. Do not be afraid and don't be condescending. No special treatment either. Acceptance by the general public would truly enable us to be more than a label to everyone and not be depersonalized by a real illness.

ANNEXES

1. **National Institutes of Mental Health—Longitudinal Analysis**

   A. NIMH Completed Lifechart 1952-2005—Prophylactic Efficacy of Valproate in a poor Responder to Lithium and Carbamazepine for Salvina Cappello

   B. NIMH Lifechart 1952-1996—Prophylactic Efficacy of Valproate in a Poor Responder to Lithium and Carbamazepine for Salvina Cappello

   C. A Page from Scholarly Journal—NIMH Lifechart 1980-1989—Prophylactic Response to Valproate in a Non-Responder to Lithium/Carbamazepine—for Salvina Cappello

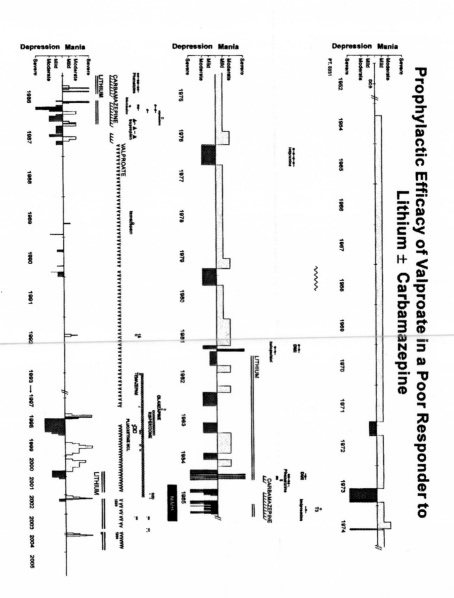

Prophylactic Efficacy of Valproate in a Poor Responder to Lithium ± Carbamazepine

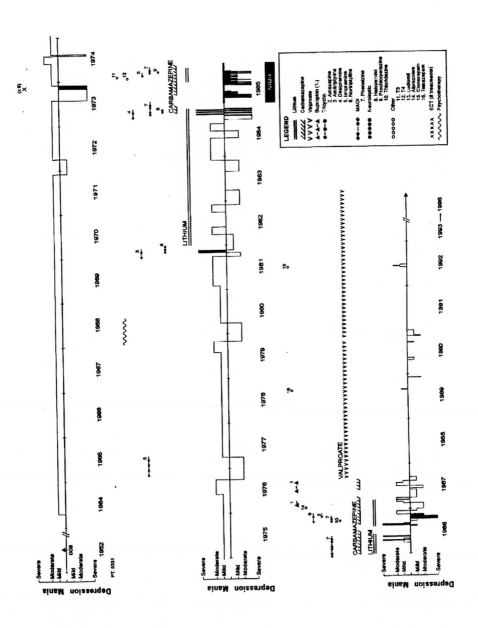

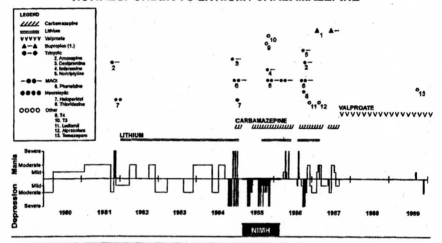

Life Chart for Salvina Cappello

PROPHYLACTIC RESPONSE TO VALPROATE IN A NONRESPONDER TO LITHIUM / CARBAMAZEPINE

After an extremely difficult course of illness with inadequate response to lithium alone and in combination with carbamazepine and a variety of antidepressant adjuncts, the patient showed a dramatic and sustained response to valproate.

Continued from page 2...

was instituted in the fall of 1987, the patient responded not only acutely with a complete remission of her manias and depressions, but has continued to remain essentially well for the last seven years.

The emergence in the last two decades of a series of anticonvulsant compounds such as carbamazepine and valproate for the treatment of bipolar disorder has brought new hope for the lithium non-responsive or lithium refractory patient. The efficacy of carbamazepine and valproate as mood stabilizers has been demonstrated in research studies and clinical practice settings and will be further investigated in the Stanley Foundation Bipolar Network together with other newer anticonvulsants thought to be potentially useful in bipolar disorder. Both carbamazepine and valproate have shown to be effective agents for the treatment of bipolar disorder, and as illustrated in the life chart, non-response to one anticonvulsant does not predict non-response to the other thus offering multiple treatment options to the patient struggling with an unstable mood disorder.

The patient whose life chart has been presented in this article has resumed a full and productive life. She gave us permission to use her life chart and case history as a message of encouragement and hope: even when there is non-response or refractoriness to some of the available mood stabilizing medications for many years, a series of alternative compounds are now available. Life-charting of the past and present course of bipolar illness will significantly assist in making informed treatment decisions.

...non-response to one anticonvulsant does not predict non-response to the other thus offering multiple treatment options to the patient struggling with an unstable mood disorder.

2. Correspondence Related to Securing Wellbutrin when it was not yet Approved

    A. Letter from Salvina Cappello with Initial Inquiry to the Drug Company. Response from Burroughs Wellcome.

    B. Response from the Federal Drug Administration after Similar Inquiry

    C. Mailgrams from my Treating Physician and Myself to Congress—I was, at this point desperate for the drug.

       We finally did get the drug for a drug trial.

Salvina Cappello

11/26/86

Burroughs Wellcomb Company
3030 Corawallese Road
Research Triangle Park
North Carolina 27709

I am writing to you to make you aware of my current medical circumstances because I
believe that you may be able to help me. I am a 34 year old female with rapid - cycling
bipolar illness. Until two years ago, my illness was not disabling and, in fact, I had a
number of accomplishments. The recurring problem in treating my current medical
condition is that my depressions are severe and not completely treated by lithium
or tegratol and the antidepressant drugs that are currently on the market repeatedly
induce me into hypomania or full blown mania. I will remain unstabilized and
disabled until this situation is resolved.

I am writing to obtain access to your drug named BUPROPRION - Wellbutrin. It has been
brought to my attention by my physician that this is the first antidepressant drug that treats the
depression, but does not induce mania. My understanding is that the FDA has not yet
approved it because it lowers the seizure threshold.   I might point out that the majority
of people for whom this drug would be useful are people with manic-depression, like myself,
and many of us are on the anti-convulsant drug - tegratol.

I am currently a patient of Dr.   G   at   University and he supports my
trial run on Wellbutrin by request of compassionate waiver.

My first preference is for him to administer the drug, but I am prepared to go anywhere
in the world to get a trial run on this drug.

Thank you in advance for your concern. I can be reached by mail at the above address and
by phone at 201-366-8566.

Burroughs Wellcome Co. 3030 Cornwallis Road
Research Triangle Park, N. C. 27709

cables & telegrams
Tabloid Raleigh, N. C.
TWX5109270915
tel. 9'9 248-3000

December 9, 1986

Ms. Salvina Cappello
P.O. Box 764
Dover, NJ 67801

Dear Ms. Cappello:

I am writing in response to your inquiry about Burroughs Wellcome Co.'s
antidepressant, Wellbutrin® (bupropion hydrochloride).

Although Wellbutrin was approved by the Food and Drug Administration in
December 1985, it was voluntarily withdrawn from the market by our Company
in March 1986 after discussions with the FDA. Wellbutrin was withdrawn
because of apparent side effects experienced by non-depressed bulimia
patients. To date, we have been unsuccessful in reaching an understanding
with the FDA about the implications of this data.

Burroughs Wellcome Co. is not conducting additional studies on Wellbutrin at
this time, and it does not seem likely that the drug will be available in
the immediate future.

We will attempt, to the best of our ability, to keep physicians fully informed
about the status of Wellbutrin. I would encourage you to have your physician,
Dr. Jackson, contact our Medical Department at (919) 248-3000 for additional
information.

Sincerely,

Lisa Reese Behrens
Consumer Relations

DEPARTMENT OF HEALTH & HUMAN SERVICES   Public Health Service

---

Food and Drug Administratio
Rockville MD 20857

Salvina Cappello

ℓ

Dear Ms. Cappello:

I am responding to your letter of November 26, 1986 that expresses your
distress about the possibility that Wellbutrin (bupropion) may not be marketed.

To begin, it is important for you to understand that the FDA has not rendered
a final decision about the marketability of Wellbutrin and it currently allows
Burroughs Wellcome to distribute the drug under a compassionate IND program to
physicians for use in patients who, like yourself, have a documented need for
it.

It is also important to understand that the FDA is fully aware of the
potential benefits that Wellbutrin may offer to selected patients. Indeed, if
the FDA had considered Wellbutrin to be simply another 'me-too'
antidepressant, it would not have approved it for marketing last year. Let me
explain.

Despite its potential advantages, Wellbutrin is a potentially dangerous drug;
at doses only slightly greater than those required to produce its
antidepressant effect, it causes an unacceptably high incidence of generalized
convulsions (seizures). A generalized convulsion is not a trivial side
effect. Depending upon the circumstances (e.g., driving a car, operating
complex machinery) in which it occurs, a seizure can cause serious injury,
even death; worse, the injury may involve others besides the the patient
taking the drug. At the very least, even a single seizure followed by full
recovery may have profound effects upon an individual's personal life; a full
and costly medical workup may be necessary, driving privileges may be lost,
etc.

Thus, a high risk of seizure is ordinarily an absolute barrier to the approval
of a new drug. However, the FDA was mindful of the problems confronting the
depressed patient unresponsive to or intolerant of existing antidepressant
treatment and an effort was made to find a way to allow Wellbutrin's marketing
under circumstances that might reduce the risk of seizure.

The FDA's initial review of the records of patients who experienced seizures
while taking Wellbutrin suggested that the risk of seizure was probably
affected by the total amount of drug given daily and the rate at which the
daily dose was changed. On the basis of this analysis, the FDA agreed to the

2

In the spring of 1986, shortly after approval had been granted but before full scale marketing of Wellbutrin had begun, additional reports of seizures occurring within the dose range recommended in the product's labeling (i.e., the supposedly safe dose range) were received. An analysis of the reports indicated that Wellbutrin might be associated with a much higher risk of seizure than earlier evidence had indicated. Both the firm and the FDA were alarmed by these findings and both agreed that additional data was needed to settle the question; clearly, there is an incidence of seizure that can not be accepted in a marketed drug product no matter how cautionary its labeling.

The decision to delay marketing and carry out a large scale clinical study to estimate the actual risk of seizure among patients taking the drug at the recommended dose was reviewed and endorsed by an independent board of experts, FDA's Psychopharmacologic Drugs Advisory Committee.

Setting up a complex study takes time and over the past five months, FDA staff and representatives of Burroughs Welcome have engaged in iterative negotiations to develop proper testing conditions and protocols. It appeared that agreement was close on all but minor issues when, in mid-September, the firm announced that it had decided to discontinue its development of Wellbutrin.

Clearly, this is an unfortunate decision and the FDA shares your hope that the it will be reconsidered. The firm has been encouraged to continue to provide Wellbutrin, under their compassionate treatment program, to physicians. You can be assured that the FDA will continue to cooperate with Burroughs Wellcome to seek to find a way to continue development of this promising drug product.

Sincerely yours,

Director
Division of Neuropharmacological
  Drug Products
Office of Drug Research and Review
Center for Drugs and Biologics

MAILGRAM SERVICE CENTER
MIDDLETOWN, VA. 22645
57AM

1-024000500700Z 01/07/07 ICS IPMMTZZ CSP NYAC
1 2129602371 MGM TDMT NEW YORK NY 01-07 0411P EST

► DR JACK GORMAN
15 WEST 81 ST
NEW YORK NY 10024

THIS IS A CONFIRMATION COPY OF THE FOLLOWING MESSAGE:

 2129602371 MGMS TDMT NEW YORK NY 43 01-07 0411P EST
ZIP
CONGRESSMAN HENRY WAXMAN
CONGRESSIONAL OFFICE BLDG
WASHINGTON DC 20515
AS A PRACTICING PSYCHIATRIST I URGE YOUR FAVORABLE CONSIDERATION OF
THE NOVEL ANTI-DEPRESSANT BUPROPRION. THIS MEDICATION IS SAFE AND
EFFECTIVE FOR PATIENTS WITH BIPOLAR DESEASE.
  JACK M GORMAN MD DEPT OF PSYCHIATRY COLUMBIA UNIV.

16:10 EST

```
ORGE CAPPELLO
 5 SOUTH MORRIS ST
'ER NJ 07801 08AM
```

```
4-0039165008 01/08/87 ICS IPMMTZZ CSP NYAB
 2013668566 MGMS TDMT DOVER NJ 298 01-08 0946A EST
```

DR JACK GORMAN
WESTSIDE PSYCHIATRICT ASSOCIATION
15 WEST 81 ST
NEW YORK NY 10024

CC: CONGRESSMAN HENRY WAXMAN
SENATOR PETE DOMENICI
DOCTOR EDWARD SCHWEIZER
DOCTOR JACK GORMAN

TO-DOCTOR FRED GOODWIN FROM NIMH AND DOCTOR ROBERT POST FROM NIMH
BY NOW YOUR AT LEAST VAGUELY UP DATED ON MY MEDICAL SITUATION BOTH
DOCTOR JACK GORMAN AND I BELIEVE THAT WELLBUTRIN IS MY ANTIDEPRESENT
STABILIZING DRUG, AND WE BOTH BELIEVE THAT IT IS LIKLEY THAT I WILL
NOT SURVIVE MUCH LONGER WITHOUT IT I SPENT 11 MONTHS AT THE NIMM AND
I WAS A VERY COOPERATIVE RESEARCH PATIENT ALTHOUGH I WAS IN A
BASELINE STATE WHEN I LEFT NIMH ON A COMBINATION OF LITHIUM, TEGRATOL
AND NARDIL - 2 MONTHS LATER I CYCLED UP INTO WHAT WOULD HAVE BEEN MY
NATURAL MILD HYPOMANIA AND THE NARDIL INDUCED ME INTO A PSYCHOTIC
MANIC BREAK. IN THE 15 YEAR HISTORY OF MY ILLNESS; THIS IS MY FIRST
PSYCHOCIC BREAK AND IT IS DRUG INDUCED. I CONTINUE TO HAVE INDUCED
BREAKS EVEN WITH THE LITHIUM TEGRATOL INSTALLED. IS THE NIMH DOING
ANYTHING ON BEHALF OF BIPOLARS TO MAKE VISIBLE THE SERIOUS SITUATION
OF INDUCED MANIAS TO CONGRESS DURING THE HEARING ON WELLBUTRIN? I AM
NOT SEEKING ATTENTION, I AM SIMPLY REACHING OUT TO THE MEDICAL
PROFESSION, PARTICULARY THOSE THAT KNOW ME, TO HELP SAVE MY LIFE AND
I KEEP HOPING THAT SOMEONE WILL HEAR ME. I AM WILLING TO RELEASE ANY
AND ALL MEDICAL RECORDS TO THE FDA OR TO THE CONGRESS IN ORDER TO GET
THIS DRUG. I AM TELEGRAMING BECAUSE I AM TO SEVERLY BIOLOGICALLY
DEPRESSED TO SPEAK BY PHONE. MY CURRENT TREATING PHYSICAN, DOCTOR
JACK GORMAN OF COLUMBIA UNIVERSITY, FEELS THAT ALL OTHER AVENUES HAVE
BEEN PURSUED AND HAVE FAILED. HE CAN BE REACHED AT (212) 9602371.
SINCERLY
    SALVINA CAPPELLO

09:47 EST

MGMCOMP

4-0039165008 01/08/87 ICS IPMMTZZ CSP NYAB
2013668566 MGMS TDMT DOVER NJ 298 01-08 0946A EST

CC: CONGRESSMAN HENRY WAXMAN
SENATOR PETE DOMENICI
DC
DC

TO-DO   FROM NIMH AND D   FROM NIMH
BY NO   IGUELY UP DATED UN MY MEDICAL SITUATION BOTH
DUC   C   AND I BELIEVE THAT WELLBUTRIN IS MY ANTIDEPRESENT
STABILIZING DRUG, AND WE BOTH BELIEVE THAT IT IS LIKLEY THAT I WILL
NOT SURVIVE MUCH LONGER WITHOUT IT I SPENT 11 MONTHS AT THE NIMH AND
I WAS A VERY COOPERATIVE RESEARCH PATIENT ALTHOUGH I WAS IN A
BASELINE STATE WHEN I LEFT NIMH ON A COMBINATION OF LITHIUM, TEGRATOL
AND NARDIL - 2 MONTHS LATER I CYCLED UP INTO WHAT WOULD HAVE BEEN MY
NATURAL MILD HYPOMANIA AND THE NARDIL INDUCED ME INTO A PSYCHOTIC
MANIC BREAK. IN THE 15 YEAR HISTORY OF MY ILLNESS, THIS IS MY FIRST
PSYCHOCIC BREAK AND IT IS DRUG INDUCED. I CONTINUE TO HAVE INDUCED
BREAKS EVEN WITH THE LITHIUM TEGRATOL INSTALLED. IS THE NIMH DOING
ANYTHING ON BEHALF OF BIPOLARS TO MAKE VISIBLE THE SERIOUS SITUATION
OF INDUCED MANIAS TO CONGRESS DURING THE HEARING ON WELLBUTRIN? I AM
NOT SEEKING ATTENTION. I AM SIMPLY REACHING OUT TO THE MEDICAL
PROFESSION, PARTICULARY THOSE THAT KNOW ME, TO HELP SAVE MY LIFE AND
I KEEP HOPING THAT SOMEONE WILL HEAR ME. I AM WILLING TO RELEASE ANY
AND ALL MEDICAL RECORDS TO THE FDA OR TO THE CONGRESS IN ORDER TO GET
THIS DRUG. I AM TELEGRAMING BECAUSE I AM TO SEVERLY BIOLOGICALLY
DEPRESSED TO SPEAK BY PHONE. MY CURRENT TREATING PHYSICAN, DOCTOR
          OF   , FEELS THAT ALL OTHER AVENUES HAVE
BEEN PURSUED AND HAVE FAILED. HE CAN BE REACHED AT
SINCERLY
    SALVINA CAPPELLO

09:47 EST

MGMCOMP

3. Letter from Previously Treating Doctor to Friends in order to help Explain Why I did some things in a Type 1 Manic Episode.

December 6, 1999

To Whom It May Concern:

I have known Ms. Salvina (Sivan) Cappello since early 1987 and in the past treated her for bipolar mood disorder, type II. Although I am no longer her treating physician, I am very familiar with her case. Ms. Cappello was one of the first people placed on Depakote for the treatment of bipolar illness and had a wonderful response, with complete stability and freedom from symptoms for 10 years.

I understand that she had two manic episodes while in Israel. I believe that these were secondary to acute situations, probably sleep deprivation. Although she does need to introduce better buffers into her lifestyle against future sleep disruptions, I have every reason to believe that she has an excellent prognosis. Ms. Cappello has responded very well to mood stabilizing medication in the past. She is a very cooperative and determined patient who always follows medical advice.

Manic episodes in bipolar patients are characterized by impaired judgement, irritability, provocative behavior and increased spending. Ms. Cappello recognized that people in this state are often offensive in speech and feels bad that she may have unintentionally offended several people while in the manic state. It is important to recognize, however, that this is a medically temporary situation and not her fundamental character.

I regard Ms. Cappello with tremendous respect. Despite her early struggles before finding the right medication, she has made notable achievements in her life. I have known her as a bright, pleasant, and engaging person and a model patient.

I hope you will take this information into consideration and that it is helpful to you.

Sincerely,

JMG:cmt

BIOGRAPHY

Salvina Cappello has an extensive professional background in media research, and especially television media research and marketing. She held key positions at a major ratings service, a television flagship network affiliate station and television production companies. She began her career in 1976 and served in various high level capacities. She has an undergraduate degree in Chinese Language and a Master's degree in Demography, the study of population statistics. Ms. Cappello was a Senior Media Consultant and most recently consulted for a network station in Israel. She has traveled worldwide with a special interest in the Middle East. She enjoys reading, walking and all kinds of people and cultures. She loves nature; the vehicle by which we can know there is a God. She also likes to write poetry.

Ms. Cappello is a member of the Depression Bipolar Support Alliance (DBSA), president and founder of its Long Beach Island Chapter, and board member of DBSA-New Jersey.

Salvina Cappello was nominated for the 2005 Eli Lilly Award.

Printed in the United States
47537LVS00004B/388-390